PHILOSOPHY

AN EYE ON THE WHOLE

Kendall Hunt
publishing company

ERIC M. RUBENSTEIN

Indiana University of Pennsylvania

Cover image © 2016 Shutterstock, Inc.

Kendall Hunt
publishing company

www.kendallhunt.com
Send all inquiries to:
4050 Westmark Drive
Dubuque, IA 52004-1840

Copyright © 2016 by Kendall Hunt Publishing Company

ISBN 978-1-4652-9889-8

Printed in the United States of America

CONTENTS

CHAPTER 1

Introduction: What Is Philosophy?

The aim of philosophy, abstractly formulated, is to understand how things in the broadest possible sense of the term hang together in the broadest possible sense of the term. Under 'things in the broadest possible sense' I include such radically different items as not only 'cabbages and kings', but numbers and duties, possibilities and finger snaps, aesthetic experience and death. To achieve success in philosophy would be, to use a contemporary turn of phrase, to 'know one's way around' with respect to all these things. . . . What is characteristic of philosophy is not a special subject-matter, but the aim of knowing one's way around with respect to the subject-matters of all the special disciplines . . . It is therefore, the 'eye on the whole' which distinguishes the philosophical enterprise.[1]

The Subject Matter of Philosophy

Chances are that you are now enrolled in your first philosophy class, perhaps out of curiosity, but more likely because it satisfies a requirement you need to graduate. But now that you are here, what do you expect? What exactly is this discipline of philosophy? If you have any associations with the field, you might think of it as one that studies "deep questions," or perhaps one of those subjects where there is no right answer, only opinions. And while it is true that philosophers themselves disagree on everything, even the nature of their chosen field, there are a few important things we can note here. Keeping those in mind as we go through the rest of this book will prove useful to you.

First, philosophy (which derives from the Greek words "philo" [love] and "sophia" [wisdom], i.e., "lover of wisdom") is unique among other disciplines because there is no specific subject matter for it to investigate. Think about other courses you might be taking—from biology to chemistry, to business law and art history. All of them have a subject matter—an area of investigation which you learn about, memorize facts about, understand the history and developments of, etc. But if you ask what the subject matter of philosophy is, you find there isn't one. Or, put perhaps slightly differently, *everything* is a potential subject for philosophical investigation. Everything. That is why there is a philosophy of language; a philosophy of science; philosophy of mind; philosophy of art; philosophy of economics; philosophy of sports; philosophy of business ethics, to name just a few. So, it would seem that if we

---

1 Wilfrid Sellars, "Philosophy and the Scientific Image of Man," *Science, Perception, and Reality*. Ridgeview Press: Atascadero, CA.

were to try and understand what philosophy is all about we can't focus on its subject matter, because nothing gets ruled out; there's a philosophy-of-anything-you-can-think-of.

Second, if there is no specific subject matter for philosophy, perhaps what makes it a distinct field is its breadth. Consider the passage quoted above from Sellars. There we find him arguing that philosophy seeks to understand how "everything" fits together. Compare that with say, sociology. In the latter, you very well may study different ways societies are organized, or factors that contribute to poverty, or of how we think about prison and punishment. But, by its very nature, sociology will limit itself to human social systems—that's why it is called "sociology." Sellars, above, however, speaks of philosophers' desire to understand not just everything, but crucially, how different things are *related to each other*. Let's quickly look at an example of this idea of investigating "how things hang together," and the idea that philosophy keeps "an eye on the whole."

Take a mundane example, say of coming home to find that your new puppy has eaten your favorite pair of shoes. Should you punish the puppy? If so, why? Well, if you were going to think through the question in a philosophical frame of mind, you will find yourself facing a range of questions, such as: What is the point of punishment in the first place? Is it to simply repay the harm one has received by harming another? (That's known as a *retributive* justification.) Or is it simply to deter similar actions in the future? If the reason for punishing the puppy is to get it to act differently in the future, is that because we are imagining the puppy being able to learn its lesson? If so, are we imagining that the puppy can understand language? Are we imagining the puppy being able to exert free will, so that once you teach it to not eat your shoes it will (sometimes) choose to act differently? Well, as soon as you ask those questions we find ourselves with other ones in the neighborhood to answer—such as what the nature of language is, and whether human beings are the only ones that can genuinely speak a language. And what exactly is free will, such that the puppy might not have it but we might? And if there are deep differences between how we treat humans and non-human animals, is that based on there being a certain essence to being human that puppies lack? What is that?

The point here is that when we approach a question from a philosophical perspective, we find ourselves facing not just that question but all the ones that are connected with it. Like a giant web of interconnected questions, concepts, theories, hypotheses, and facts. Part of what makes philosophy different then, is *how broad its scope is*: everything is a potential subject for philosophical investigation, as we've seen, and now we also see that philosophy seeks to understand how all the different pieces fit together. Doing philosophy is like putting together a giant puzzle, piece by piece. Or, to change metaphors, it is like learning one's way around a detailed map—of seeing how all the different roads and towns and rivers and railroad tracks all fit together.

In seeking to understand the nature of philosophy there is a third point worth exploring. Notice throughout our discussions we've made reference to a "philosophical investigation" or "philosophical perspective" on a subject (where, again, it seems anything can be subjected to that kind of investigation). Yet what exactly is it to investigates things in a *philosophical* manner? Answering that question takes us perhaps to the heart of the philosophical project, namely, the *method* of inquiry involved.

The Method of Philosophy

Here is where we find what is perhaps most distinctive of philosophy, namely the way it goes about exploring and investigating an issue. It is true that philosophy sometimes asks questions that are "deep" and which other disciplines don't ask, say about the meaning of life, or about whether we have obligations to non-human animals. But regardless of the topic or question being asked, philosophy is arguably different because of its method. What is that method? One way to think about it is that the philosophical method involves a rigorous, patient, thorough intellectual exploration of *all* sides of an issue. Philosophers like to move slowly and carefully through a topic. They are not satisfied with quick, superficial answers. In fact, sometimes philosophy is often more focused on figuring out what the right *questions* are to ask, as opposed to the answers. And all that takes time and energy. But the payoff is multi-faceted. For in thinking slowly and clearly about a subject, examining all sides and perspectives, one gains a deeper understanding of the subject matter. Just as importantly, one develops certain skills, skills that are beneficial whether you are studying more philosophy or doing any other cognitive task, namely, learning the virtues of patience, of self-control, of being able to stay with a topic and not be sidetracked or distracted by irrelevant factors.

Now, admittedly, this is still a fairly vague characterization of what philosophy is. We know something about how broad its investigations go, and we know something about how it investigates things. The way this book is going to work, however, is not by spending more time telling you what philosophy is. Instead, you will learn what philosophy is by actually doing it.

In the coming chapters, we will focus on a number of the most famous of philosophical topics, wrestling with the questions and ideas themselves. In other words, you are going to learn what philosophy is by being a philosopher. And if all goes well, as it should, at the end you will have learned not only important skills, such as how to read a text carefully, you will have also learned what it is to think philosophically about a topic. And because, as the quotation from Sellars reminds us, philosophers care about how things "hang together," you will also have begun the process of learning how to keep an eye on the whole.

A crucial aspect of learning to keep an eye on the whole is to reflect upon, even discover, some of our most deeply held beliefs. These may be beliefs we hold about who we are as individuals, about others, including family members, about how the world works, whether there is life after death, whether we have a soul, and countless other beliefs. Often these deeply seated beliefs inform and guide our actions. Philosophers work to uncover these deeply held beliefs, the kinds that don't typically show up in ordinary conversation. And once we discover what some of our deepest held beliefs are, we can attempt to evaluate them. This, however, is not an easy thing to do, on multiple levels. First, because these beliefs are so deep, forming the fabric of who we are, it is hard to critically evaluate them, as they may be quite abstract or difficult to get a firm grasp of. The second reason is that because such beliefs are important to us, it can be threatening to call them into question. In the next chapter we will examine several of such deeply held beliefs, and see how they stand up to scrutiny.

Thousands of years ago, Socrates famously remarked that the "unreflective life is not worth living." At least part of what he meant was that it is better to grapple, in an intellectually honest way, with the beliefs we hold, hoping we can understand them better and reach clarity about not only what we do believe, but what we also *should* believe. He thought that the very process of reflecting upon our beliefs, especially the deeply held, important ones, was an important part of being human. And it is no accident, of course, that in a college textbook on philosophy that we find ourselves beginning the process of discovering and reflecting upon these special beliefs. For it is often when people are of college age, and/or at college itself, that they have a chance to reflect upon the beliefs they grew up with, and to decide whether those beliefs are ones that they should continue to hold onto as they get older. This is at least part of what Socrates had in mind when he spoke of the "reflective life"—of discovering what some of our deepest held beliefs are, and of deciding whether we should continue to believe them because we were taught them by our parents, our communities, our friends, etc., or whether we should decide for ourselves what we ought to and will believe.

In the next chapter we begin this process. We will also begin to get clearer about how it is that philosophers evaluate beliefs themselves, so that we can reach an understanding of what is involved in both keeping and also rejecting or modifying those beliefs that play such an important part in how we think about ourselves and the world.

One final point, one that addresses how to read philosophical texts, such as this one. The way philosophers tend to work is that they will present an argument (or, relatedly, some support or defense) for a belief. That belief is then subjected to scrutiny, and possible problems with the belief, and importantly, also the alleged *support* or *reasons for* the belief might then be called into question. Then, in response to those questions, a defender of the original belief tries to rebut the objections that come from this imagined opponent. Then, perhaps, they go another round, with the opponent trying to respond to the attempted rebuttal of his/her original objections, and so on. The result of this extended back and forth is that reading philosophy becomes like reading a dialogue or a debate. That can make it hard to keep track of what's going on, and whether a given point is being offered in defense of the original theory or is part of showing that theory to be wrong. To help, consider working out a roadmap for yourself as you read. Write out what the belief is that is being debated. See if you can figure out what is being said on *behalf* of the belief. Then, imagine a different person arguing that the belief is wrong, and see if you can write out what the imagined opponent would say is *wrong* about the belief. *Then*, see what the original defender of the idea or belief says in reply to their opponent. In other words, try to keep track of when we are *defending* a belief and when we are *criticizing* it. If you can do that, and keep track of the back and forths, you will have far more success. And the more you do it, the easier it will become.

CHAPTER 2

Reason and Faith

In this chapter we are going to discuss religion and faith. Now, typically when people talk about faith, they mean faith in God. And there have been countless philosophy books written over the ages devoted to such questions as whether God exists, about what God is like, about the connection between God and human free will, about why bad things happen if the world was created by an all-loving being, to name just a few. While we will make passing reference to some of those questions, they will not be the focus in this chapter. Instead, we will be asking about the phenomenon of *faith* itself—which, while it includes talk of faith in God, will not be limited to only that kind of faith. We will also look to understand the complex relationship between reason and faith. But before we turn to those difficult issues, there is a more fundamental issue we should explore. This will continue our earlier discussions of what philosophy is all about, and will be a good opportunity to be more specific about what I've called the *method of philosophy*.

We will begin by talking about beliefs we hold (no matter what their subject matter is), and what one famous philosopher referred to as our "intellectual obligations" toward our beliefs. That will help us think more clearly about what is involved in evaluating a belief we have, and how to decide whether any particular belief is one we should continue to hold on to, whether it needs to be revised, or perhaps, even rejected from the group of beliefs that inform our views about ourselves and our world. Once we have spent time thinking about these "intellectual obligations," we will be in a position to return to the nature of faith, including religious faith, again, with the goal of having at least a richer, fuller understanding of what faith is, what it is not, and how it is connected with belief and action.

In a broader context, this discussion will be one of many opportunities to see how different issues are connected, and thus what is involved in "keeping an eye on the whole," the theme and title of this very book.

Belief and Evidence, Part I

Everyone is familiar with the idea of having *moral* obligations—of there being actions that are required of us to perform, even when we don't particularly want to. (In fact, as we'll see in later chapters, one way of understanding ethics or morality is to see it is as commanding us to perform certain actions whether we want to or not.) Thus while the idea of "obligation" is not new, the concept of an "intellectual obligation" may be. The philosopher William Clifford argued that in virtue of our being creatures of a certain type—beings who can think and reason—that we have obligations, not just for how we should act, but also for what we *ought to believe*.

In particular, Clifford argued that we have an obligation to believe *only those things for which there is sufficient evidence*. We'll leave it open for now what exactly counts as sufficient evidence, but the idea is that we shouldn't believe something unless there is good support for that belief. Now the evidence or support can come in lots of different forms—it could be in the form of a mathematical proof; or it could be that we have reliable evidence from our senses, or that the belief is one that shows itself to be true as soon as we stop to think about it. What's important, for Clifford, is the idea that we owe it to ourselves to only believe those things for which there is sufficient evidence—we should only believe things which we can provide good support or backing for. And if there is not such support to be found? Well, Clifford thinks we should reject that belief and stop believing it.

In speaking of our having these intellectual obligations, Clifford is saying that we are somehow doing something wrong if we continue to hold onto beliefs which do not have the appropriate evidence or support. A word philosophers often use here is "justification": that we should believe only those things for which we have *justification*—something that makes that belief well-supported or grounded.

Using this idea of *justification*, we can revisit our earlier, somewhat vague descriptions of what philosophy is, now seeing it as the discipline that requires us to sort through our deepest beliefs and to literally prune from that stockpile of beliefs those for which we don't have sufficient evidence or justification. If that requires us to modify or give up a belief near and dear to us, so be it. Thus the reflective person, now bringing Socrates back into the picture, aims to figure out what can be justified or supported, and seeks to construct a worldview which contains only well-supported or justified beliefs.

This isn't a crazy idea, by any means, and perhaps is simply an extension of what we already think is true and important. If I told you there were tiny, invisible gremlins in my watch, and that they are responsible for making the hands move, you'd think I was guilty of making a serious mistake. You'd think that I shouldn't maintain that view about the gremlins and the watch unless I had some kind of evidence. And if the evidence I gave you for thinking there are such gremlins was that it came to me in a dream, you'd reject that as just silly—for dreams are not a good source of evidence or support or justification. In short, I bet you'd believe I was being rather foolish or irrational in continuing to hold that belief about gremlins without any *good* evidence to support it.

Now, of course, that is a silly example. But the general idea still holds, and Clifford wants us to apply the point to *all* areas of our cognitive life—to sort out which beliefs truly do have genuine evidence supporting them, and which ones don't. What's more, he thinks that when we find beliefs that don't have the requisite support or evidence that we should stop believing them. This general idea of believing only those things for which we have good evidence is sometimes called the "ethics of belief"; that just as we have ethical obligations to do certain actions, we also have a similar kind of ethical obligation to only believe what we have sufficient evidence for.

What we're now going to do is apply this idea of the "ethics of belief" to a particular set of beliefs, namely ones that involve religion and faith. That will give us one way, an important way, to begin thinking about faith, religion, and God. Crucially, like all of the topics we will explore in this book, we are merely going to begin a discussion or dialogue. Philosophy as a discipline has been around for nearly 2,500 years. So of course we can't settle everything (or maybe even anything) in a book of this length. But we can get started, figuring out what the important questions to ask are, and to begin to grapple with what might make one answer better than another. Even those small steps are important ones, and count as progress.

Belief and Evidence, Part II: Does God Exist?

Think of some of the beliefs we have for which we *do think* we have sufficient evidence, of the kind Clifford requires we have. Beliefs about the color of regular size objects before our eyes might be a good example—say, "There is an orange chair in front of me." In general, we tend to think of our *senses* as providing support or justification for many of our beliefs about the world. Other kinds of support might come from using our powers of reasoning, as when we are doing complicated mathematical problems. That then gives us two kinds of ways of supporting or justifying our beliefs: using our senses and using our reason. And though we will return in a later chapter to the question of whether we can truly depend on our senses, let us assume for now that we can.

What happens when we seek to provide evidence or support or justification for the belief that God exists? Many, many people believe that God exists. And that belief is often a very important one in people's lives. To a philosopher, that makes it all the more pressing for us to determine whether there is support or evidence for that belief. So, can our senses provide the kind of support that Clifford tells us to find for the belief that God exists? At least for many religions, it seems it cannot. For according to many religious traditions, God is simply not the kind of being who has a physical body. But without a physical body it seems we cannot use our senses to see or touch God, and thus cannot be used to support the claim that God exists. We can't see or feel God, that is, at least directly, since God isn't physical in the way that tables and chairs are.

What about our powers of reasoning? In the history of philosophy there is a very long, important tradition which attempts to demonstrate that religious beliefs, say about God, are ones that can be supported by reason. This process, what is sometimes known as "natural religion" tries to prove that God exists by providing detailed arguments or proofs, similar to how one might prove a mathematical theorem to be true. For our purposes here we won't explore those famous arguments, simply noting the names of the most famous three: the Ontological Argument; the Cosmological Argument; and the Design Argument.

Understanding how those arguments work is important to understanding the history of philosophy (and the philosophy of religions). We won't explore those arguments here, however, but not just because of the amount of space it will take. Rather, we won't for two other reasons. First, the arguments that try to prove that God exists are often thought to be not sufficiently compelling as to convince someone who doesn't already believe in God in the first place. And thus many people think that neither the senses or even reason can provide evidence for God's existence. Second, and more importantly for our purposes, many people think there is something wrong with the very project of trying to prove that God exists in the first place—that somehow the very idea of *proving* God exists is wrong-headed. Perhaps this is because people often think that religious beliefs depend on *faith*, where faith and reason are thought to somehow be incompatible. That is, many think the whole point of religion is to draw upon people's faith, not their powers of reason. It is this point I want you to explore further.

Notice that if you decide that one shouldn't even try to prove that God exists, because you have faith, it seems that you are ignoring Clifford's command that we make sure we believe only things we have sufficient evidence for. Now if you think Clifford, in general, is on to something important, namely that as rational beings we should make sure we believe things for which we have good evidence or support, then to *not* apply that requirement to religious belief seems troubling. Especially when religious belief, as noted, seems to be so important to so many people. In other words, if there's *any* belief we should have good reasons to believe is true, it would certainly seem like religious beliefs are ones we should scrutinize. So to not even try to support, say, the belief that God exists, on the grounds that you have *faith that God exists*, is to disregard Clifford's important general point about needing to support all our beliefs. If we are to make an exception for religious beliefs it seems we at least need to explain *why* they don't require support while all others do.

Belief and Faith

As I noted, there is a very long tradition, one that includes some of the most important religious thinkers, who think that religious beliefs can be supported by use of reason, say by using those three kinds of arguments I listed above. What I'm interested in here, though, is the response which says that religious belief is *different*, and different in a way that makes it not necessary to meet Clifford's standards. For perhaps the proper response to Clifford is to say that when it comes to religious belief, it *is* different, and doesn't need to be justified. In particular, I'm interested in understanding what happens when people say things like, "I don't need to have evidence or proof that God exists, because I have faith." How should we understand that kind of remark? Why, as I asked above, is religious belief exempt from the Clifford's ethics of belief, which requires all beliefs to be supported? If you think religious belief is different, what exactly is the difference? And what do you mean when you say that you don't need evidence because you have faith? How should we understand this idea of *faith*?

Let us briefly explore a few ways it might be understood, with an eye to seeing if these ways of invoking one's faith are ultimately helpful or not. This is a difficult issue, and so we can only hope to scratch the surface. But let us at least try.

First, when someone says "I don't need evidence because I have faith," we might take them to mean that the whole point of faith is to be able to believe in something in the absence of evidence. The fact that God, say, cannot be observed, requires *not* that we stop believing that God exists, but instead recognize that this is a special case where we are supposed to believe in the *absence* of evidence. If we had evidence, you might say, there wouldn't be any point in having faith.

Second, perhaps when we talk about having faith, we mean that faith is its own, special way of supporting our beliefs. On this view, faith is what makes it OK to hold that belief, as faith is a special kind of relationship we can have to God or to the truth.

Third, perhaps when we talk about faith we are actually doing something very different than it appears. Notice that when we have spoken of justifying our beliefs, we've spoken of beliefs using the word "that," as in "believing *that* it is raining," or "belief *that* there is a table in front of me." And we might think that when we start talking about faith that we are still thinking about sentences where we are claiming "that something is true." But, on this third suggestion, maybe this is all a mistake. For maybe what is going on when we speak of faith is that we are speaking of having faith *in God*, not faith *that God exists*. We aren't trying to prove that something is true, but instead are speaking of something like faith *in* a person, not truths about that person, say *that* they are tall or old.

Let us try to evaluate these three different proposals, starting with the last one. That is the hardest one, perhaps. The idea behind it, again, is that when we began with Clifford's talk of "intellectual obligations," we focused on trying to support or find evidence in our beliefs *that* things are a certain way. And when we transitioned to talking about faith and God it might seem as if we are still trying to do the same thing, namely, to find evidence or support for our faith *that* God exists or faith *that* God is good. But perhaps this misses the whole point of faith—for when people speak of faith they are speaking about their faith in a special being, where this faith is something like trust. If that is right, maybe the very idea of trying to find support for religious belief is misguided, as we're not trying to justify or support our beliefs at all, as what we're really talking about is having trust or faith in a special being, namely God.

Now, while I think this is an important idea to consider, I think there are important questions that have to be asked about it. Namely, usually when we talk about having faith *in* a person, where we mean something like trusting that person, we tend to think that trust has to be earned, or at the minimum, that we have to reasons why it makes sense to trust that person. After all, many people are not trustworthy, and we usually think that either someone has to earn our trust, or that there has to be some type of reason or evidence to lead us to think that person is deserving of our trust. Now, if trust in God is to be understood as similar to trust in a person, don't we have the same kinds of issues as we did before? That is, don't we still need to find some kind of evidence or support that God, similar to a person, is deserving of trust? If so, what is the basis for this trust? The same problem as before seems to arise, as it doesn't seem like God is the kind of being we can observe acting and then form a judgment about his/her reliability and whether God is worthy of trust. The same problem of lack of evidence shows up, that is, whether we are talking about *faith in God* or *faith that God exists*.

Let's go back to our earlier ideas, where we somehow tried to avoid having to support or justify our beliefs about God by noting that the point of faith is to believe in the absence of evidence. As we saw, one question that arises for this view is that it is unclear why, when it comes to God, we are suddenly able to avoid Clifford's demands that we believe only those things that we have sufficient evidence for. Maybe belief that God exists is different than belief that trees do. But we can't just assume so. We need to find a principled reason for treating religious beliefs differently, and so for not subjecting them to the same standards that we do the rest of our beliefs.

Consider the following silly example. Suppose I start off by saying, "I believe that there are gremlins in my watch." You, having learned about Clifford, say in response, "Well, that belief has to be based on evidence. And if we can't find any evidence for the existence of those gremlins, you need to give up that belief about the existence of those gremlins." Now imagine that my reply to you goes as follows: "OK, you are right, I don't have any evidence for my belief that there are gremlins, but I have faith that there are." In this example, we're imagining someone admitting that they can't back up their belief in gremlins, but that they also don't want to give up that belief. So, instead of revising or dropping that belief, they try to shelter it, as it were, by claiming that they don't need evidence, they just need faith. They are, in other words, trying to keep the beliefs they already have, but trying to make them immune from Clifford's standards by claiming they have faith that the gremlins exist.

Thinking about this silly example can be useful. If you are convinced by Clifford that one needs evidence for one's beliefs, you know that these beliefs about the gremlins don't get a free pass, as it were, just because someone claims that they have faith that they exist. "Faith" is not a magic word which lets us believe anything we want to.

Having recognized that, here's the challenge: In the gremlin case we know something has gone wrong. What happens, though, when instead of speaking of gremlins we simply substitute the word "God." Then we would be imagining a situation where someone admits that they don't have evidence or support for the claim that God exists. And if we now invoke faith? Does "I have faith that God exists" stand in any better light than "I have faith that gremlins exist"?

Of course there is no gremlin-based religion. But is that relevant? A thousand or a million people proclaiming they have faith that gremlins exist doesn't change our initial problem does it? Namely the problem of seeing if there is anything which can provide the kind of support for beliefs about God that Clifford thinks appropriate. Comparing the gremlin case to beliefs about God is not intended to make the latter seem silly. It is done with an eye to understanding exactly what the relation is between faith, belief, evidence, and religion.

In fact, through all of these back and forth exchanges, there has been one overarching point. It is this: there is nothing wrong with speaking of or relying on faith. As philosophers, however, we should make sure we understand what is happening when we use that important word, "faith." Faith is a special part of many people's lives. But that makes it all the more important to understand what faith is. The discussions to this point have tried to raise at least some of the questions about faith that one should try to answer.

A final point. As is clear in the above, there are lots of different things being said, and it can be confusing because at one moment the text seems to be supporting a view and in the next breath seems to be suggesting it is false. That can be confusing. Try to think of philosophy as a dialogue—an extended, ongoing exchange of ideas, where there is always more to say. A good analogy here is how things work in a courtroom. Imagine a courtroom where a defense attorney imagines not only what they will say on behalf of their client, but will also imagine what the other side is going to say, and so they prepare a reply for how they will defend their client against what the other side is likely to say. The defense lawyer, in other words, is arguing with herself in the simple sense that she is trying to imagine both sides of a debate, and thinks about what each side will say when confronted with an opposing view.

That is what we are doing here. We are taking each belief we focus on as important, and we are subjecting it to intense scrutiny—thinking about what is to be said *for* that belief and what is to be said *against* it. Ultimately, the goal is to find and keep those beliefs which survive this intense scrutiny. Put differently, as said above, there's an important sense in which Clifford's view about beliefs and evidence is really a model for how philosophy itself works. We're sorting out the well-supported beliefs from the unsupported ones. And to the extent that you yourself are taking part in this scrutinizing of beliefs, you are already doing philosophy.

We've explored in this chapter some difficult but important questions about reason and faith. And we've spoken of the importance of having support for one's beliefs. In the next chapter we will go even further, seeking to understand what knowledge in general is, and whether we really do ever have good reasons for thinking we *do* know how the world is.

CHAPTER 3

The Nature of Knowledge

The "JTB" Analysis of Knowledge

One of the most enduring themes throughout the history of philosophy focuses on the nature and limits of knowledge. Are humans capable of knowing every truth there is? Do we only have different opinions about a subject but never knowledge? What is the source of the knowledge we do have? Remembering our last chapter, we might ask about whether it is possible for humans to know that God exists, or whether it is possible to know God's mind or God's plan.

All of these questions presuppose we understand what *knowledge* actually is. But that leaves unaddressed such important questions as: What is the nature of knowledge? And how does knowledge differ from mere opinion or speculation? Until we can arrive at an understanding of what knowledge is, it will be impossible to address the larger themes about the limits of knowledge and questions about what things we can have knowledge of. So, in this chapter we will begin by examining a traditional account of the nature of knowledge. With a definition in hand, we'll then see if we do in fact have knowledge of the things we take ourselves to in fact know. Along the way we'll see that there are serious hurdles we have to overcome in order to claim that we do in fact have knowledge of even simple things—such as knowledge that you are seated right now, with a book before you.

To give this chapter a historical grounding, we are going to approach the question about the nature and possibility of knowledge using some of the ideas of one of philosophy's most famous—René Descartes. In fact, we'll even name one of the views in the forthcoming debate after him. Let us say that "Cartesian Skepticism" is the view that we have no knowledge about the way the world is, and that the only knowledge we have is about our thoughts, ideas, sensations, perceptions, and the like. On that view, we have no knowledge, about whether any of our thoughts about the world are true or whether any of our perceptions accurately reflect how the world is. This skepticism is a very pessimistic position, as it denies that we have knowledge of many of the things we take ourselves to know. Now the historical figure, Descartes, advanced this idea of "Cartesian Skepticism" as a challenge, one that forced himself and his readers to get clear about what exactly we do know and how. Ultimately, Descartes thought he could overcome this skepticism and regain genuine knowledge of how the world is. We won't follow Descartes' entire journey, only parts of it. But we'll review enough of his thoughts, combined with some more contemporary reflections, to get a sense of how hard it can be to prove that we have any genuine knowledge at all.

To begin, let us try to define what actual knowledge involves, leaving for later the question of whether we have it and what we have knowledge of. Let's see, in other words, what the difference is between knowledge and opinion or mere belief, and then later see if we do have knowledge or only opinion.

The first thing to note is that for our purposes, we are speaking about knowledge that something is the case. We do (or don't) know *that* 2 + 3 = 5; or *that* there is a green tree outside my window. Notice the use of the word "that." It indicates a proposition or fact that we supposedly know. What we'll be exploring is whether it is possible for us to know those facts or propositions. We are not, in other words, speaking of knowledge of *who* someone is or knowledge about *how* to do something. To make things a bit more concise, let us use a variable, just like in math, to stand in for any of those propositions or facts we mentioned.

That is, we can say, "Sally knows that p" where "p" stands for any proposition, such as "2 + 2 = 4" or "Grass is green." This will also help us keep in mind how general our discussions are. We are focused on the nature of knowledge itself, not the knowledge of one field or another.

So, what is needed for us to say Sally—or, to get even more concise we can just use "S" to stand for our subject—S knows that p? What is the difference between Sally's *knowing* that the sun is hot and Sally merely having the *opinion* that it is?

Let use an example to get started. Does it make sense to say that Sally knows that the moon is made of cheese? No. Why not? Because the moon is not made of cheese. Thus the first thing we might note is that it isn't possible for Sally, or anyone, to know what isn't true. We can have knowledge only of what is true. That, in turn, gives us our first condition for having genuine knowledge. We'll put it as:

S knows that p when (and only when):
i)   P is true.

That's a good step, but clearly not enough to distinguish knowledge from opinion. Here's something that's missing but which is so obvious it might be hard to notice—but we're trying to be careful here and get everything out in the open, to make sure we avoid taking anything for granted. Notice that so far, we listed only the fact or proposition, what we're calling *p*, and we have the person we hope has some knowledge. But a fact's being true can't count as knowledge for S *unless S is in some way actually thinking about that fact*. The subject, our thinker, has to be in some type of cognitive relation to that proposition, p, for it even be an opinion of hers, much less genuine knowledge. So let us add to the above, making it clear that a necessary step toward S knowing that p is that S at least be thinking or believing that p. We'll put that, combined with the above as:

S knows that p when (and only when):
i)   P is true.
ii) S believes p.

Yet even if we have both (i) and (ii), that still doesn't seem to count as knowledge for Sally. Why not? Because we can also have opinions or beliefs that are true, but which we still wouldn't want to claim count as knowledge. For instance, consider one of those contests where you are asked to say how many gumballs there are in a giant jar. Suppose you looked briefly at the jar and said that there are 3,234 inside. And suppose you actually are right. Would this count as knowledge? Did you know that there are 3,234 gumballs in the jar? Or, rather, would we claim that you simply got lucky with your belief or opinion, as it just happened to be true? You didn't *know* it, rather, you merely had a true opinion. If that's right, what is missing?

Here it might help to think back to our discussions of Clifford. Our beliefs should have support or evidence for them. Or, to use the more technical term, they should be *justified*. The problem with the gumball case is that though we have a true opinion, we have no actual support or evidence to back up our belief—that is why we called it a lucky guess. And that gives us what traditionally has been thought of as the third and final condition needed for us to have knowledge, namely,

S knows that p when (and only when):
i)   P is true.
ii)   S believes p.
iii) P is justified.

That is, knowledge requires we have true beliefs that we actually have support or evidence or justification for. In the gumball case, suppose someone asked Sally how she knew there were that many inside. If she answered, "Well, I counted them out and then placed them back inside the jar, and made sure no one tinkered with the jar," we would likely say that her belief now *does* have evidence or support, and that she is justified in her belief. And because the belief is true, she really does know that there are 3,234 balls inside. But if she had said, "Well, 3,234 is just my favorite number, and that is why I picked it," we wouldn't hold that her belief was justified. It was just a very lucky guess.

So now we at least know what we are aiming for when we try to decide whether someone knows that something is true—we'll ask whether they have a justified, true belief. (The acronym used here is that this is the *JTB analysis of knowledge*—justified, true belief—and it appears in philosophy as early as in one of Plato's dialogues.)

A Regress Argument

We are soon going to bring Descartes into the discussion, and explore a line of thinking that calls into question our right to claim we truly know anything. To set the stage for him, though, we'll explore a famous problem that arises when we try to think through the JTB analysis of knowledge we just developed. This is what we'll call the "Problem of the Infinite Regress."

Remember that for us to know something (to know *that p*), there must be grounds or evidence or support for our belief that p is true. Crucially, that support or evidence is no help to us in supporting the belief in question if we don't also know the evidence exists and supports our belief. For instance, to know that it is raining requires there be something that supports or justifies our belief that it is raining. A good example of support would be that the ground is wet. But we have to *know* that the ground is wet if we are going to be able to claim that *we* know it is raining.

In other words, to know p requires that we also know *something else*—we have to know *that the support for p is true*. That is, we now need to know something else, which we can call r, if we are to have any hope of knowing *p*. So, knowing p requires we already know r. But now the same issue arises: We need to have evidence/support/ justification for our knowledge of r. And *that* brings in *yet another* belief.

Stepping back, we can see that we've found a threat to our knowing any one particular fact. Namely to know any one particular thing seems to require we know an infinite number of things. (Make sure you can see how repeated application of the problem in the previous paragraph generates an *infinite* number of beliefs).

Unfortunately, humans don't seem to be able to know an infinite number of things, nor to think through an infinite number of steps—r justifies s which justifies t which justifies m, which justifies o . . . repeated indefinitely. This repeating pattern—a regress—threatens our ability to claim we know anything. For, again, it suggests that to know (and justify) one single belief, requires we know and be able to justify an infinite number of beliefs. But we don't have the time to do that (as it would seemingly take an infinite amount of time) nor can we think about an infinite number of beliefs.

How do we get out of this infinite, vicious regress? (It is called "vicious" because it is a harmful regress, one that threatens our ability to plausibly claim we know anything.)

One way out, it seems, would be to find a belief that has a special status: one that is *self-justifying*. Such a belief would be one that doesn't need *another* belief to justify it. And, it is a belief that as soon as we think about it, we recognize it as justified. If we could find that special belief we'd be able to halt the regress and have a basic, foundational belief that we could rest all other beliefs on. In contemporary philosophy, this approach to the regress problem is known as "Foundationalism." (There are other strategies available for addressing the regress, but focusing on Foundationalism will help us bring in Descartes more easily.)

Descartes and Three Stages of Doubt

We've left the discussion so far as the search for a special kind of belief, namely one that is self- justifying, one which could halt the regress of justification we saw threatens our ability to know anything.

We can now pivot to the philosophical struggles of Descartes, who wrote in the seventeenth century, and who is the inspiration for both the regress problem, and a solution to it. He's also the source for that idea mentioned before, "Cartesian Skepticism," which denies we have any knowledge of how the world is. Let us see how Descartes both creates, or, rather, *discovers* the problem and tries to solve it.

Descartes, in his famous, *Meditations on First Philosophy,* often just known as *The Meditations,* wants to find a way to justify or support the newly emerging scientific picture of reality that philosophers and scientists were developing. He thought it crucial to put such scientific beliefs on a solid foundation—much like a house is as only stable as its foundations. Descartes took it upon himself to find a belief or set of beliefs which could be the ultimate ground or support for all of our knowledge, including the new scientific view of the world (one that was beginning to replace the old Aristotelian understanding).

His way of proceeding was quite radical, in that he decided that for any belief to be considered a candidate for a foundational belief it had to pass a high threshold.

Namely, if any belief or set of beliefs were merely possible to doubt, then he would consider those beliefs *false,* and reject them as candidates for that special foundational belief. That radical, or *hyperbolic method of doubt,* would ensure that we avoided any error, as it would exclude any proposed bit of knowledge that was even possible to doubt, thus making sure our foundations of knowledge were as solid as possible.

To make things simpler, for our purposes, let us use Descartes' project of radical doubt as a method of finding the self-justifying belief *we* were looking for. That is, we'll follow Descartes' search for a belief that can't be doubted, and consider that belief as potentially one that is the self-justifying belief *we* are seeking. So, once we've found what Descartes considers a belief beyond doubt, we'll ask whether it is self-justifying. If it is, we'll have found a self-justifying belief, one that dovetails with Descartes' own search for a foundational belief that can't even be possibly doubted.

So, in review, we've briefly seen how Descartes approaches this problem of what we know, namely, by his not letting himself believe anything to be true unless it is incapable of being doubted. And we said that a belief that couldn't even be doubted would be a good candidate for that self-justifying belief we have been looking for, one that stops the regress.

Now in order to find that special belief (the one that can't be doubted and is self-justifying), Descartes systematically calls into question all of the beliefs we have about the world, and sees if there is way to doubt them. If *nothing* survives this doubting process the result would be that we don't know anything about ourselves or the world. That pessimistic conclusion we called Cartesian Skepticism—that we don't know anything about the nature of the world or ourselves. We're trying to avoid that pessimistic conclusion. As for Descartes, he proceeded by creating a doubting process that has three distinct stages of doubt, where as we go through the levels of doubt, each one gives us increasingly more serious worries about whether we know anything.

Where do we begin? Since so many of our beliefs about the world are based on our senses, Descartes thought we should ask whether we have reason to trust our senses and the beliefs based on them. This gives us our first stage of doubt:

Sensory Deception

At this level of doubt, we note that sometimes our senses lead us astray. Given that, some of our beliefs shouldn't be considered as knowledge, as it is possible to doubt them.

Which beliefs? Well, if you are looking at something very small or very far away, it is possible to doubt whether you are seeing things as they really are. And given that we aren't going to let into our foundational beliefs ones that can be doubted, it seems we should exclude beliefs based on our senses where we are sensing something very small or far away.

But while our senses lead us astray when it comes to small or distant objects, aren't there lots of sensory based beliefs that are about things right before our eyes? What reason do we have to doubt those beliefs—say, that you are seated right now, or that the sun is setting outside your window? The next stage of doubt, where we find reasons to doubt even those sense-based beliefs, is where things get really interesting.

The Dream Argument

Can we trust our senses about things that are right before our eyes? What could Descartes possibly give as a reason to doubt *those* beliefs?

Consider this: Say you believe, based on your senses, that you are sitting at your desk reading this book. Then, given the sensory evidence, we might think you are in a position to claim you know you are sitting at your desk. But suppose instead of you actually sitting at the desk, what is happening right now is that you are in fact having a vivid dream, and *in the dream* you are sitting at the desk reading a book, though in fact you are laying in bed sleeping. If so, then you can't be said to know that you are sitting at the desk because you aren't, and as we've seen, you can't have knowledge of things that aren't true. So to rightly now claim you know that you are sitting by your desk, you have to know that you are not dreaming, and then you can rely on what your senses are telling you. But here's the hard part: Are you in a position to claim you know you are *not* dreaming right now? Do you know you are actually awake, not merely dreaming?

Notice that sometimes we have dreams that are so vivid and realistic that when we wake up we are shocked to discover we had only been dreaming. Couldn't that be what's happening now? That you are about to wake up from a dream and say, "Wow, I just had this crazy dream about philosophy, where in the dream I was asked whether I was dreaming!" Can you be sure you are awake now and not dreaming, and not just about to wake up from this philosophy dream? Descartes thinks we can't tell—that there are no signs to distinguish being away from dreaming at any given moment.

True, once we awaken we can talk about how dreams are often less coherent than real life, or that things are fuzzy in dreams, or that events happen in unusual orders. But when you are in the midst of a dream you are taken in by it, so to speak. That's why when you wake up you can find yourself shocked and disoriented. We're now simply asking: Is it possible that you could be dreaming all this right now, and are about to wake up and say, "This philosophy class is now invading my dreams!" If you can't rule out that possibility, then it seems you can't claim to know you are sitting at your desk.

In other words, knowing you are sitting at your desk requires knowing you are not dreaming. But you don't and can't have knowledge that right now you are not dreaming. So, logically, you can't know that you are sitting at your desk. And thus every sensory based belief you have can be called into question—they could all be the product or part of a dream you are having right now.

If that is right, then maybe we can't trust any of our basic sensory beliefs. That's pretty radical. Is there anything else we could possibly know in this bleak scenario?

The Evil Genius

You might think that even if we are dreaming, there are still some things we could know, say that triangles exist and have three sides, or that $2 + 2 = 4$ is true, regardless of whether we are dreaming or not. Or perhaps some other basic belief about how things are might be a candidate for knowledge. But in this third stage, Descartes is going to give us reasons for doubting *all* of our beliefs.

Imagine that there is only your mind—that you have no physical body, there are no trees or cars or other people or anything. But yet you believe there are such things. Why do you believe there are these things? Well, because perhaps there is a super powerful being that is planting all of those thoughts and sensations of there seeming to exist trees and cars directly into your mind. You have those experiences and beliefs not because there is an external world that resembles your ideas about how the world is. There is just this Evil Deceiver causing you to have a systematic, vivid hallucination—one that is complete and never lets up. You are just being fed a steady stream of misleading data.

(If it helps to update this scenario a bit, imagine your brain is hooked up to a computer, and the computer is sending you tons of signals directly to your brain, causing you to have a coherent experience of a world, even though in reality there is just your brain and the computer.)

Could you tell the difference between experiencing trees that are really there versus merely having those experiences because the sensations/ideas/thoughts about those trees are planted in your mind by this evil deceiver [See Figure 3.1]?

The problem, it seems, is that all we ever have to go on, when trying to understand what is real, are our own thoughts, sensations, ideas, experiences. But from the "inside"—how things seem to us—those experiences could just as well be a systematic illusion as they could of the real world. This is the Cartesian Skepticism we've spoken of, where it is now threatening to call into question our belief about whether there is even an external world of trees and the like.

This is a depressing place to land. For now it seems that we can't be certain of anything, and that we could all be living a systematic illusion. In that case we really wouldn't know anything.

Is there any hope for us? Is there anything we can know? Any belief that could be justified? And, remember, we've also been looking for a special belief—one that is self- justifying—something that we know which could serve as the starting place for all of our alleged knowledge of how things are. We need something that can't be doubted, something we could know even if there were this evil deceiver, and something that when we think about would justify itself. That would be truly a foundational belief. And it would be the start of reclaiming our right to claim we do have knowledge of something.

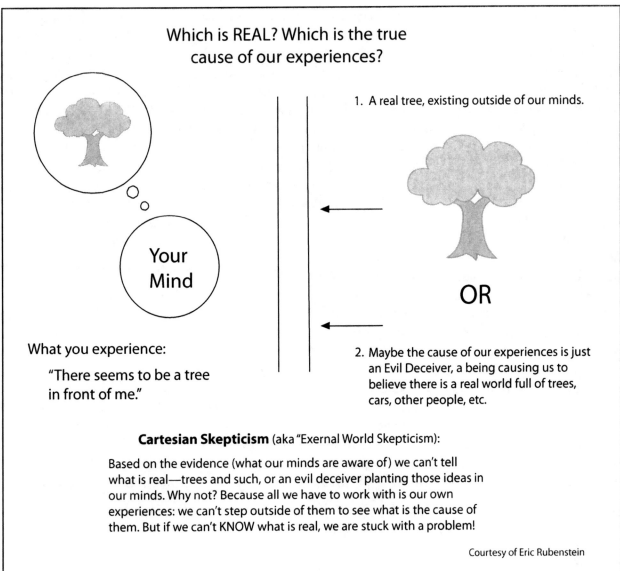

Which is REAL? Which is the true cause of our experiences?

Your Mind

1. A real tree, existing outside of our minds.

OR

What you experience:

"There seems to be a tree in front of me."

2. Maybe the cause of our experiences is just an Evil Deceiver, a being causing us to believe there is a real world full of trees, cars, other people, etc.

Cartesian Skepticism (aka "Exernal World Skepticism):

Based on the evidence (what our minds are aware of) we can't tell what is real—trees and such, or an evil deceiver planting those ideas in our minds. Why not? Because all we have to work with is our own experiences: we can't step outside of them to see what is the cause of them. But if we can't KNOW what is real, we are stuck with a problem!

Courtesy of Eric Rubenstein

Figure 3.1

One Foundational Belief

We've now arrived at the same place Descartes does, despairing whether there is anything we can know and whether we can trust our senses to give us knowledge at all. Descartes himself spends the rest of his book, *The Meditations,* trying to regain his right to claim he has knowledge of how the world is. We won't go through all of his steps, but will simply explore his starting point, which involves what is probably the most famous line in all of philosophy, one that almost everyone seems to have heard of, even if they don't know the context or significance.

Descartes is famous for saying: "I think therefore I am." Now Descartes doesn't actually use those exact words, but says something close, namely, "I know that I exist whenever I am thinking." What is so important about that famous line?

Well, think about the claim that "I exist whenever I am thinking." Surely if you are thinking there must be something of *you* that is doing the thinking. Even if you didn't have a body, you'd *still* have your mind that is thinking that thought. And what happens if you try to *doubt* that belief—the belief that you exist when you are thinking? Well, doubting is a kind of thinking, so even when you are doubting you are *thinking*. And if you are thinking you must be around, in some fashion, to be able to do the thinking. Even trying to doubt the belief ends up just confirming its truth it seems. So, again, what justifies you in the belief that you exist when you are thinking? You just have to think about it! For when you think about it you are again finding out you exist.

If this is right, then we do know something. And even if it doesn't tell us everything we want to know, it is a starting point. Descartes himself uses this as his foundational belief, again: "I exist whenever I am thinking." And from there he tries to rebuild the more complex structure of knowledge we hope to have about the world. For our purposes what is significant is that this one belief is something that is true and that we can know to be true even if there is an evil deceiver. That being can't make us not exist when we are thinking. Yes, *what* we are thinking about might be misguided, but there can be no doubt that we exist when we are thinking. This is known as "the cogito"—that we can be sure we exist whenever we are thinking. ("Cogito" is Latin, roughly meaning "to think.")

As a result, Descartes now has a way to stop that regress we explored above, and has found something we can be sure of. Again, what justifies us in thinking that it is true that we exist when we are thinking? It seems we just have to think about it. And in thinking about it we support or justify that belief: We prove we exist when we are thinking every time we think! That's a crucial starting point. And while we won't go through how he proves the rest of the story, we know how it begins.

Notice, in conclusion, how much we still can't be sure we know: we don't know we have a physical body, we don't know there are other people, we don't know there are trees or the sky or space or anything. And we still don't know whether we can trust our senses. The project of determining what we know and how we know it is in fact very much alive even today. The branch of philosophy that focuses on the nature and limits of knowledge is known as *epistemology*. We've now gotten our first taste of it.

CHAPTER 4

Death

Death and Dying

It may seem depressing to have a whole chapter on the subject of death. But death is a crucial part of humanity's experience. It is often noted that humans are the only beings that are aware of their own mortality. How we think about death influences how we think and live our lives. Even leaving aside the role of death in religion, and beliefs in an afterlife, humans struggle with death—the death of a loved one, the fear of dying, the difficult decisions faced when a friend is terminally ill, the morality of suicide, to name a few. We'll take a small step toward thinking clearly about death here, asking some basic questions about death and how we should think about our own (inevitable) death.

If you were to make a list of the worst things in the world, or the worst things that could happen to you, death would likely be on the list. And probably pretty high up. That suggests a good opening question: Is death actually a bad thing? If so, what makes it bad? Related to those questions is another: Is death something we should fear?

In order to make progress on these questions, we should make an important distinction. Namely, there is the state of actually being dead on the one hand, and there is the process of dying on the other. Now for the sake of the arguments and discussions to come, by "death" I mean the total cessation of you. I am stipulating, for our discussions, that once your body and brain are lifeless that that is the end of your existence. I am ruling out, in other words, the possibility of an afterlife, or that you have something like a soul which is able to survive your bodily death. Whether we do have souls, and whether they can survive the death of our bodies is an important philosophical issue in its own right. But we can only address so many issues at once.

We're hoping to think clearly about death in this chapter. The only way we can do that is to take seriously the idea that death is the total, complete end of you. With that in mind, we can put the distinction we made between *being dead* and the *process of dying* to work. First, let us be clear about what is involved in actually being dead, as that is the harder of the two to grasp. A common mistake people make when they think about their being dead is that they imagine it as an experience they will have—such as imagining yourself at your own funeral. But, of course, if you are truly dead, you will have no such experiences. In fact, given how we've come to understand or define death here, when you are dead there are no experiences at all. There is nothing that being dead is like. Why? Because death is the end of you, and as such there is no experiencing being dead. If there is no you, when you are dead, then there can't be any experiences you have.

Now what often trips people up is that they confuse the state of being dead (where there are no experiences) with the process of dying. And the process of dying can, unfortunately, be extremely unpleasant or painful. But if we keep in mind that distinction, we can say that while the process of dying can be painful, the state of actually being dead cannot. For as we've said, there is no you, once you are dead, to be having that painful experience.

Should We Fear Death?

Given all of that, how should we now think about our own death? Is it something we should fear? As we begin to ponder this question, make sure not to confuse *being dead* with the process of *dying*. For being dead is not like getting a painful root canal, which you might be afraid of before it happens. Being dead, as we've said, is not an experience you live through or which you can think back on later. So, while it does make sense to fear the process of dying—which is why people often say they hope they die peacefully in their sleep—it isn't clear at all why we would fear *being dead*.

Now it might be tempting to say that you fear death, being dead that is, because it is unknown, and we tend to be afraid of unfamiliar things. But notice the mistake in that line of reasoning. It again presumes that there is something like being dead—a way it is to be dead which you can be afraid of. But that again is to forget that as we keep saying, being dead means there is no experiencing at all. And so it can't be that being dead is an unfamiliar experience we could understandably be afraid of. Perhaps we are again confusing a fear of what dying might be like with the actual state of being dead.

Another way you might try to explain why you fear death is that perhaps when you contemplate your own death, you think about all that you will miss and the pain that will come to people who cared about you. Plus, it is just hard to imagine the world going on without us. For whenever we try to imagine the world going on, we always put ourselves into the picture, seeing the world from a particular vantage point. This is similar to how we imagine our own funeral—imagining there is a place we are sitting or observing things from.

But the main point still holds. True, there is much that you will miss out on once you are dead. But reflecting on all that you will miss on seems like it would trigger feelings of sadness and maybe even anger about what you'll miss out on. What still seems hard to understand is where the feeling of *fear* comes from. Why should we fear death? If we think clearly about what it is to be dead, and distinguish that from the process of dying, perhaps we can liberate ourselves from that fear altogether. That doesn't mean we have to welcome being dead, but perhaps we can reason our way toward not being afraid of it. That would be an important realization; even a consolation.

But maybe you've not given up yet in trying to make sense of why we fear death. Maybe you fear death because you don't know *when* it will happen. That's true—for while we all know we will die, we rarely know when. But what exactly is the fear about in this case? To my mind, when I'm afraid of when something is going to happen it is because I'm not wanting to have that experience at all, and the fear stems from not knowing when to be prepared for it: Not knowing when I'm going to have that unpleasant experience, and being afraid of getting caught off guard or unprepared. This, however, seems to be making the same mistake again. For if death is not an experience we have, then once again, it is hard to understand why we fear it. Death is not like being unprepared for an emergency root canal that we later can think back on and say "that was bad!" It just isn't an experience for us at all. And so, again, it isn't clear why we would fear it. There isn't, in other words, an experience to be prepared or unprepared for, since there is no experience at all when you are dead.

Perhaps the following diagram will help explain why it so hard to think about death as not being an experience we have. For perhaps we are confusing, at root, two different ways of thinking about

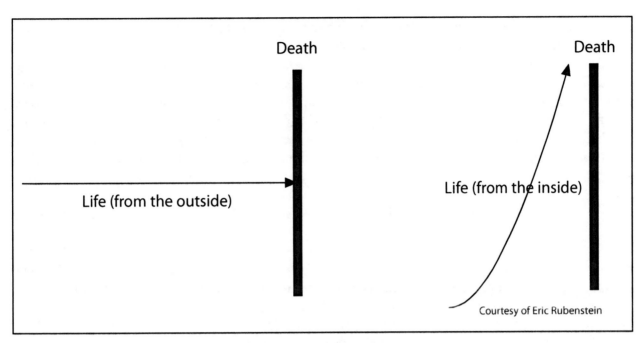

Courtesy of Eric Rubenstein

Figure 4.1

death. On the one hand, we experience the world from our own vantage point, having experiences and seeing the world from our own perspective. Let's call this "experience from the inside." From the inside, death is never something we experience, and in that way is like an asymptote in mathematics—a line that gets closer and closer to a given point but never touches it. From the outside, however, viewing others, we can think of their death as more like the end of a line segment. But because we always experience things from our own perspective, we might confuse seeing things from the inside with seeing them from the outside. When we imagine things "from the outside" we are no longer talking about what we experience. And that is perhaps why we find ourselves thinking of death as something we will go through. But from the inside, we will just keep having experience after experience until they stop. But those experiences never will be of death, they will be of being alive, even as we get closer and closer to death (see Figure 4.1).

Having gone this far, and seeing that perhaps there is no reason to fear death, it might be possible to go a further step and wonder whether death is even a bad thing in the first place. In pursuing that line of reasoning we'll be tracing some of the arguments that come from the ancient philosopher Epicurus, who believed that death is neither something to be feared or even bad in itself. Why should we think death is not bad, since, as we've noticed, most people are inclined to think of death as the worst thing in the world?

Is Death a Bad Thing?

As we continue our discussion, keep in mind we are asking about whether it makes sense for you to fear your own death, and whether it makes sense to think of your own death as a bad thing.

That is importantly different than thinking about whether your being dead is bad for others, as it most certainly will be for those who knew and cared about you. Just as it would be bad for you if someone you loved happened to die. But what we're focusing on here is whether being dead is actually a bad thing for the person who had died. In order to answer that question, and to see what Epicurus had in mind when he claimed that death is not a bad thing, we need to step back and ask a more general question, namely, one about what makes bad things bad.

Suppose you drew up a list of all the bad things you could think of. And then I asked you to go through that list, and for each one, keep asking you: "what is bad about *that*?" For instance, if you think lying is bad, I would ask you why it is bad. You might reply that it unfair to someone else to keep the truth from them. And to that I'll ask again, "what is bad about *that*?" Here you might answer that it is bad because treating people unfairly is bad. You can see where I'm going, perhaps—asking the "what is bad about that?" question over and over. Ultimately, in our example, I think we'd eventually say something like, "being unfair to people is bad because it makes them unhappy or causes them pain." Now if you were to go through the list you made of bad things, I suspect all of them would eventually lead you to the same conclusion: bad things are bad because they are either painful themselves or are the cause of pain.

Let's take that thesis, that bad things are bad because of their connection with pain, and apply it to the case of being dead. Remember what we said above: being dead is not an experience you have, because it is the cessation of you and all of your experiencing. If so, then being dead can't be a painful experience because it isn't an experience at all. And here we get a surprising conclusion: Since death is not painful, and all bad things involve pain, it seems that death is not a bad thing at all.

To say it again, if bad things are bad because of their connection with pain, and death involves no pain, at least for us, then it isn't a bad thing. Death, in other words, according to this argument isn't in fact something bad. That doesn't mean it is good, but it does mean it isn't a bad thing. And if Epicurus is right in this argument, then we've learned something else important about death—it is neither bad *nor* to be feared. If this argument is a good one, we might find ourselves thinking very differently about our lives, even feeling liberated again from the worry that someday we will die.

But is his reasoning persuasive? Are you convinced? Let us see if we can find a way to reply to Epicurus' argument, by seeing if there are any flaws in it. To do so, let's make his argument explicit, making all the steps clear the way we would if we were doing a proof in geometry, say. The steps we've taken seem to include the following line of reasoning, where we are thinking about whether being dead is bad for the person who is dead, not their family or friends, etc:

i)   Bad things are bad because they are painful or the cause of pain.
ii) Death (the state of being dead) is not an experience we have.
iii) Therefore, death isn't painful for us or the cause of pain for us.
iv) Therefore, death is not a bad thing.

Now one way we can critique an argument is to see whether the starting points of the argument, what are known as *premises*, are true. In this argument, the first premise, (i) is doing much of the work, as it is telling us that bad things owe their badness to pain. Is it possible for us to find a reason to think that is false?

Say a friend tells you she will go watch a new movie with you, one you both are excited to see. And then you find out that she went without you. That seems to be a bad thing. But it also doesn't obviously involve any pain for you. What's bad about this scenario is that you missed out on a good experience—seeing the movie with your friend. Likewise, perhaps what is bad about death is that you'll miss out on good stuff—be it loved ones getting married or seeing your grandchildren, or falling in love, etc. That is, we can think of various things that are bad but don't obviously involve pain. So, perhaps the first step in our argument above is just wrong. And if that step is wrong then the argument of Epicurus isn't a good one, and that means he has not proven that death is not bad.

Are you convinced by this critique of the argument? Go back to the movie example. You missed out on the movie, and that seems like a bad thing. We said that it was bad because it involved missing something good. But is it possible that what really makes it bad is that you were disappointed? Or that you felt hurt that your friend broke a promise? If so, then we're back to our original point: we have another example of something that is bad because of its connection with pain—in this case the disappointment or feeling hurt by the broken promise.

Returning to the example of death, it seems the real challenge left is to see if you can find a reason that being dead is bad, without making the badness of death somehow linked to something painful. If you can do that, then you've got a good way to not take Epicurus' argument seriously. I'll leave it to you to see if you can find such a reason for thinking death is bad but not because of its connection with pain. (Here's a tough issue to resolve that is relevant: Is the absence of a pleasurable thing itself a kind of pain? Is missing out on the pleasure of falling in love for example—the absence of pleasure— itself painful?)

If Death Is Bad, Should We Hope to Live Forever?

We've raised difficult issues and questions above. Let us take a fresh start on a related topic by supposing that we aren't convinced by Epicurus, and that we continue to think that death is a bad thing. Well, if death *is* a bad thing, then the seeming solution is to simply *not die*. Immortality, in other words, would seem like it must be a good thing. But, as you might anticipate, we'll soon see that things aren't so clear. Here we will draw on a famous argument made by a contemporary philosopher, Bernard Williams, who thinks immortality is not a good thing at all. Let's see why, first, and then see where we end up. For we might find ourselves in the peculiar position of thinking death is bad but, having thought about Williams, *also* thinking that living forever is not good. If we think both of those, then it is hard to know what to say: what do we really want, if it isn't to die nor to live forever? That ends up being a difficult question, one we will return to. But first, for now, let us see why Williams thinks living forever is not a good thing.

Think of things that you want or have desires for. These will span a wide range, all the way from a desire for a cheeseburger to a desire to help others. (You might even take the time to write down some of those desires on a piece of paper so you can examine them and see for yourself which ones are more important than others.)

Now Williams thinks that among the various desires we have, some of them are more basic than others—what he calls "fundamental desires." What makes a desire a special, "fundamental desire" is that it gives you a reason to live. As for non-fundamental desires we should think of them as follows. Other desires you may have are ones that you happen to have because you are *already alive*, but don't on their own give you a reason *to live*. So, having a desire for a cheeseburger is probably not a desire that gives you a reason to live, but is simply a desire you have because you are alive.

Let us now focus on those fundamental desires. Yes, they give us a reason to live. But the key question we will ask about them is this: How long can any fundamental desire continue to give you a reason to live?

The reason this is a pressing question is because we are imagining ourselves now living forever. Forever is a long time, to put it mildly. It isn't 5,000 years we are talking about, or 500,000, or 5 million. It is forever, as in, there is no end. It is hard for us to grasp perhaps how long a time span we are considering, for whenever you imagine a particular number of years of being alive, that will be just a drop in the bucket of an eternal or immortal life.

With that in mind, now think back to those fundamental desires. Could they sustain you for such a long period of time? For example, if helping others is one of your fundamental desires, imagine yourself doing that for 50,000 years. Do you think you'll get tired of helping others after that amount of time? That it will simply become boring? That, in essence, is what Williams thinks is the problem with living forever: given enough time, any activity will cease to be interesting enough to give you a reason to live. The problem with immortality, he thinks, is that, ironically, we'll eventually become bored to death.

Now perhaps you might imagine moving from one fundamental desire to another. Say, you'll work on being a musician, and spend 20,000 years learning to be the best at every instrument. Then, you'll work on learning about history, and do that for 5,000 years. But then what? Remember that that amount of time is a tiny amount, relative to living *forever*. Is there any particular desire you could have that you wouldn't eventually become bored trying to satisfy? Williams thinks that if you really think through how much time we're talking about, that you'll end up agreeing that living forever seems not so appealing.

Here's another way to think about it. Suppose you were told that you not only were going to live forever, but that you *couldn't* die—that you were unable to be killed or get old or sick. At first you might think that was great news. But if you think through what you'd actually do with yourself every-day for eternity, you might end up thinking of it as more of a curse than as a good thing. Wouldn't you want a way to opt out, as it were? A way to not be forced to live forever?

So those are some reasons Williams thinks living forever is not ultimately a good thing. Notice there are lots of questions we've not even begun to consider, such as whether other people in your life would get to live forever or whether it would be only you. If they did live forever along with you, do you think your relationships would survive 50,000, 100,000, a million years together? What about your very own self? What age shall you be? Do you get older at all? Do you want to live forever, but only under certain circumstances, such as being healthy and having money and loved ones around you? Pick whichever version of the story you want and there is still that fundamental question about you, yourself: Do you think you would get tired of your own thought patterns and reactions after a million years? After ten million?

Clearly there are many questions left to be asked about living forever. But we've seen at least a glimpse of why Williams is so pessimistic. Suppose he is correct, and that living forever is not a good thing. And suppose we stick with the view most people have, even having considered Epicurus, that death is a bad thing. Now what? If death is bad, but living forever is also bad, what is the solution? If you could write out the script of your own life, spelling out how long you would live, what would you choose? Would you want 100 years? 1,000? 10,000? The difficulty you may face in figuring out what the answer for you would be is telling, as it shines light on both how important issues of death are, but also how little we actually understand our own lives. Being able to at least think about what we want, even if we can't get it, would be a significant achievement it seems.

CHAPTER 5

Free Will

Why the Debate Matters

One of the most fundamental activities humans engage in is categorizing or cataloguing the world. We look for similarities among things and put them in one category or group, and contrast them with items that have different sets of qualities. Even before we start doing philosophy we tend to distinguish human beings from other kinds of things, including other living things. What is the basis for our putting humans in one group and not including rocks, plants, and lions in the group? No doubt there are many things that distinguish humans from other things, but a central feature we think humans have is what philosophers call "free will." Now exactly what is free will is a question we'll explore in the pages that follow. But roughly, for now, we think of ourselves as being free in a way that we don't think rocks are. We tend to think of ourselves as having a degree of control over lives, though certainly not total control. And that control is perhaps part of what we mean when we say we are free or have free will. Rocks and plants, on the other hand, just follow the laws of nature and are pushed and pulled by the various forces acting on them, without much room for control, much less deliberation about how they will act.

In this chapter we will explore one of the deepest and oldest of questions asked about humans' alleged free will, namely: What exactly do we mean when we say that we have free will, and are we in fact truly free? We'll see that there are three different views that have been advanced for understanding the nature of humans and the ways we are and are not similar to the rest of the world. But before we delve into those positions, and begin to tackle the difficult questions they raise, we should step back a bit and think about why it would matter if we are free or not.

One reason we might give is that it matters to us when we evaluate someone's behavior whether we think they acted freely or not. Now without taking a stand yet on what it means to say someone did act freely we can still appreciate the significance. Think about how things work in a court of law, for instance. If someone is on trial for committing a horrible crime, but we discover that the person had no control over their actions, say because they were suffering from a mental illness, we very well might have a different opinion about whether they should be punished (or how severely they should be) than if we thought their actions were truly free.

Likewise, we tend not to praise people for things they had no control over—such as how tall they are. Think of how odd it is to praise someone for being tall, compared with praising them for having studied hard or worked out in the gym regularly.

In general then, it seems we tend to praise and blame people for actions they have control over, or what we might call "free action," as opposed to ones they didn't have control over. Think now about what the point of our penal system is—why we lock people up for crimes they have been convicted of doing. Why do we punish people? Here it is might be helpful to notice the words we use to name and describe prisons. They are often referred to as "correctional facilities." Why? Part of the answer is that we think of prisons as places where people's behavior can be corrected, and thus part of the reason for punishing them in the first place is to try and get them to change their behavior. That is why people who are appealing for parole are asked about whether they have rehabilitated themselves—whether they have learned their lesson and reformed their behavior such that they no longer pose a threat to others.

Of course there are other reasons we may have for punishing people, including simply wanting to remove them from communities so that they no longer pose a threat. Or because we think if someone does harm another that they should suffer a similar kind of pain. That's what some call a "retributivist" justification for punishment, as opposed to punishing someone as a way of deterring others from doing similar actions, or to help reform them. Even if we stick with the idea that the point of punishment is to reform people, we can think of that itself in different ways. Think about how you condition your dog to wait till it is taken for a walk, instead of peeing on your carpet when it feels the urge. You shaped its behavior with a combination of positive and negative reinforcements, the kinds and methods of which you might study in a psychology class. So too, prisons could be understood as "reforming" people's behavior by reinforcing good behavior and discouraging bad—that their behavior is deliberately shaped and molded. But another way of understanding people being reformed is to imagine them as having control over the actions, and eventually coming to choose certain ways of being over others, such that they learn to leave their bad ways behind them.

Why we punish, praise, and blame people for what they do is itself a very large issue, one studied by sociologists, criminologists, philosophers, and others. Relevant to those debates is how we think about humans and the control they do or don't have over their own actions. How we view this issue of control is relevant to how we view people's actions and what we think the appropriate response should be. So, as we go through the following pages, where we will at times be exploring very abstract and complex issues and debates, it is important to keep in mind some of the ways in which these debates have real-world, practical effects and implications.

Sending people to prison is just one of many examples of it mattering how we understand people and their actions, and whether they acted freely. What we'll now do is begin to explore more deeply what it is to be free, why some people think we actually are not free, despite our wanting to view ourselves that way, and how such freedom is possible (assuming we actually have it).

Determinism and Free Will, Part I

Here's an important general remark to keep in mind as you continue to get better at doing philosophy: sometimes the best (and maybe only) way to understand a difficult concept is by comparing or contrasting it with its opposite. If we want to understand what it is to be free, for instance, it will be helpful to have in mind an understanding of the opposite of being free. And here we will start with what is known as "determinism." When we say someone or something is *determined*, we don't mean that in the ordinary sense, where someone is really set on achieving a goal or are fully committed and resolved to achieving something. We mean something very different.

To help see what we mean, think about the laws of physics (or science more generally), and the relationship between cause and effect. Once a given event (cause) happens, we tend to think there is only one possible outcome (effect). Consider striking a match. To simplify, take all the elements that are present when you (successfully) strike a match: the match is dry, the red strip on the matchbox isn't ripped or wet, you struck the match at the proper angle with the proper force. Take all of those facts and simply call them "event A." When A happens what do we expect the outcome to be? The match will light. Call that event B. In the typical case, we think that once A happens (as cause) there is one and only one possible outcome or effect, namely B, the match lights. Or think of your holding a pen over your head and event A being the opening of your fingers (where we will again include all of the background facts into that event, such as that the pen isn't tied to the ceiling by invisible wires, or that you're not in outer space where there is no gravity.) In such a case, A (opening your fingers) leads to one and only one outcome or effect, B, namely that the pen falls.

Instead of speaking of cause and effect, we can use a different term and say that in such cases, event A *determines* event B. That simply means that when A happens there is one and only one possible outcome. And, crucially, that is how we think the physical world works. It just chugs along, following the laws of chemistry or physics or biology, with each event bringing about the next event. And that second event then brings about the next one, and so on. To introduce some new terminology, we might say that when A *determines* B, that means that A's happening closes off all possibilities besides B. That just means that when A happens there is one and only one possible outcome, namely B. A picture of this situation might look like this:

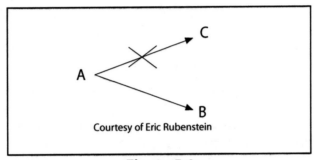

Courtesy of Eric Rubenstein

Figure 5.1

In this figure, we have A occurring, and only one possible outcome, B. C is crossed off because it isn't possible for it to happen, once A does. Strike the match and it must light; open your fingers and the pen must fall. So, again, given A, there is one and only one subsequent event, B, and that one has to happen, given that A did.

Let's stick with this just a bit longer before moving to the question of what "free will" means. For it is important to head off a possible misunderstanding. When we say that B had to happen, say that the pen had to fall, what we mean in this example was that it had to fall *because A had happened*. That is different from saying that the pen had to fall, no matter what. Here, in other words, is whether sometimes people confuse one event determining another with the idea of something being *fated* to happen.

When we say something happened by fate, that seems to mean that it had to happen no matter what happened before it. This is what we often encounter in Greek tragedies, such as the famous story of Oedipus. He was fated to kill his father and marry his mother, goes the story, where no matter how hard people tried to avoid that outcome, it had to happen, no matter what. But that is very different from saying that something had to happen only because some particular event happened to have happened first, which caused it. If we were going to draw a picture of what fate (or "fatalism") looks like, it might look like this, where all paths lead to the event, and so it had to happen, no matter what happened before.

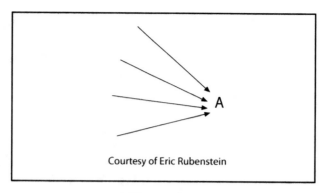

Courtesy of Eric Rubenstein

Figure 5.2

That is very different from saying something had to happen because a particular event happened first and was its cause, as we saw in Figure 5.1.

For our purposes, we are focusing solely on the relation of determinism, where we say that one event determines another such that when the first (A) happens, it makes it necessary for B to occur. Put in the other direction, B had to happen because A did, and it very well wouldn't have happened had it not been for A's happening. See how that is different from speaking of fate?

Now that we have an understanding of what determinism is, we can begin to discuss the concept of free will. Now the next point is particularly important. I mentioned that there are three positions or views that people have defended on the question of human free will. That might surprise you, because you might think the only debate is whether humans are free or are determined. As we'll see, it is more complicated than that. What makes it more complicated is that there are two different kinds of debates actually at work. One of the debates will be over what the best definition is for "free will," and the other will be a debate about whether humans actually are free (given your choice of definition). These two different debates are what makes the whole topic complicated, as we'll have to keep track of which debate we are having, and try to work on just one at a time.

For comparison, think about the definition of knowledge we explored above. We saw that the best way to define "knowledge" was as "true belief which is justified." But that was just a point about how to define the concept. It was saying, in essence, knowledge is better defined that way than it is to define it as "strongly held opinion." But even if the best definition of knowledge is *justified true belief*, that on its own doesn't prove that we do have any knowledge. Remember how hard we had to work to prove we actually do have knowledge, ruling out all of Descartes' skeptical threats. But with that definition we knew what we were looking for, and we knew what it would take to have genuine knowledge. Relatedly, part of what we'll do in this chapter is figure out (and debate) what the best definition of "freedom" is. But even if we figure out what the best definition is, that doesn't prove we have it. It just shows us what we are looking for.

With that in mind, we can give our first (of two) definitions of free will as one that says, "Free will is the opposite of being determined." And since the essence of determinism was that closing off of other possible outcomes, this first definition of free will in turn means something like, "When a person has free will, there is more than one possible outcome for how they will act." In other words, this way of understanding free will is one that involves saying that unlike rocks and chemical in a test tube, human beings have choices for what they will do.

To see this, let's use that example of the match being struck (A) and its lighting (B). Imagine watching it happen. Now, imagine it were possible to rewind the world, as if it were just backing up a movie you were watching to an earlier scene. Then let it play again. If the match hits the matchbook with the same velocity at the same angle, with both being as dry as before—that is, we completely redo event A, what is the outcome? Of course it will be event B—the match will light. That was what we meant when we spoke of one event determining another—once A happens there is one and only one possible outcome, namely, event B.

But now bring humans into the picture. Imagine event A is a person holding a lit cigar. And suppose the next event is B, where the person takes a puff on that cigar. So, A happened, and then B happened. Now let us "rewind" the universe as we did before. A happens. Does that mean that B will now HAVE to happen? Or is it possible that the person looks at the cigar and stubs it out? Or that they give the cigar to someone else? Yes, according to common sense, it does seem possible that things could play out these different ways. Why? Because we tend to think of humans as having choices. They can decide, as in this case, whether they want to smoke the cigar or not. And this having of a choice is exactly our first way of understanding what free will is. Using the language from above, we can say that when a person has free will the happening—event A (holding the lit cigar)—does not close off other possibilities. That is, there is more than one possible thing that could happen next—in this case C and B are both possible.

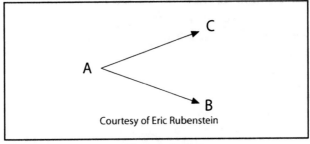
Courtesy of Eric Rubenstein

Figure 5.3

Here's a crucial point: We've not said humans *do* have free will. Rather, we've just said something about what the word means: that one way to define "free will" is to see it as the opposite of what we mean by the word "determinism." In fact, they are so opposed to each other that we can give this definition of "free will" a name, and we'll call it the "incompatibilist" definition of "free will." In other words, the definitions can't both be true of the same thing: if the definition of "free will" we've given describes something accurately, then it doesn't make sense to say it is determined, and vice versa.

Again, we've not yet said whether human beings are determined or not. We're simply working on defining the terms. In the next section we'll look at a view which says that the term which does best describe us is in fact "determined," not "free." But for now we're simply noting that how we define "free" makes it not possible for something to be free and determined, as their definitions exclude each other.

Determinism and Free Will, Part II: Hard Determinism

Having gotten clear on the definitions of the key terms, it is time to wrestle with the question you've been waiting for: Which, if any, of those definitions is actually true of human beings and how they work? The first position we will discuss is called "Hard Determinism." It thinks that human beings are always determined, including when it comes to the thoughts and feelings we have. One action, or thought, has only one possible consequence, and each human being's thinking and acting is simply the playing out of a long chain of causes and effects, where at each point there is no room for things to go other than one way. And, since on this view (call it HD for short), to be free requires that open possibility of choice we were just discussing, where it is not possible for something to be both determined and free, we can conclude we are not free. Again, according to HD, we are determined, and so we are not free. Free will, on that view, is just an illusion.

Putting this into a little argument might make it easier for us to keep track of HD and how it differs from the other positions.

1) Human beings, including their thoughts and feelings and actions, are always determined.
2) Free will is incompatible with determinism.
3) Therefore, human beings are never free.

Now before we go deeper into the reasons that HD gives for its view, in particular, why it thinks (1) is a true description of us, we should appreciate how radical the conclusion (3) truly is. What HD is saying is that human beings are never free, never have genuine choices or options, and thus that free will is an illusion.

That's a radical conclusion to reach, and if true would require that we re-conceive our own behavior and that of others. No longer would be able to hold people responsible for their actions, it seems, as no one truly has any choice or control over what they do. But as we saw before, to be able to praise or blame someone for their actions seems to presuppose they acted freely, that they had a genuine option or alternative way to act. All of that is denied by the Hard Determinist.

But why should we accept such a radical conclusion, one that goes so strongly against common sense? Here it will be helpful to look at that three-step argument we outlined above. Step 2 is where we defined "free will" as requiring open or alternative possibilities—that confronted with a situation that there were at least two different ways one could have acted. So far, it seems, that is a pretty good definition of "free will," and one that most people seem to agree with. (Though we will revisit this point later.) So, step (2) so far looks plausible. That means that the first step, (1), is also doing a lot of important work. Why should we accept the claim that human beings are determined?

Here the HD will try to convince us that human beings are ultimately just complicated bundles of matter—of flesh and blood and bone, of neurons and skin, etc. And all of those things, and the systems that they comprise—kidneys, intestines, brains, are all subject to the deterministic laws of the natural world. Just as we saw when we talked about striking matches or dropping pens, we thought of the physical world as governed by laws of cause and effect. Such laws, we saw, are deterministic. And while we might not always know what the outcome would be, say if we put two substances in a test tube together, we expect that there is only one possible outcome, because those substances and their reactions are governed by the deterministic laws of cause and effect, laws that do not leave any room for multiple outcomes.

But aren't we different, you might ask? We have thoughts and feeling and sensations. And we grow up in different surroundings and cultures and come to have our own unique values and character traits. To all of that, however, HD will simply agree, and point out that who we are is a product of our genetics, our surroundings, our culture, etc. And all of that can go into forming us as the individuals we are. But having said that, what we're shown is simply that we are very complex creatures. But even though we are complex we are still subject to the same laws that govern the rest of the natural world. And that means that every thought in your head is determined by the previous one, and the one you are having now, combined with facts about your character, genetics, and the context you find yourself in, determines what the next thought will be. So even when you are having the thought, "I'm going to choose to not smoke that cigar," that very thought (and the action that does/does not go with it) is simply determined as well by all of those complicated facts about you.

So, again, HD can be understood as arguing that because we are made of the same stuff as the rest of the physical world, we are thus subject to the very same laws that control how that stuff behaves. Those laws are deterministic, and thus everything that happens is determined. And that now includes us.

Soft Determinism

Now many people bristle at HD. We want to believe we have free will, that we have choices, that we have control over our actions. HD denies all of that. If we want to find a way to avoid this view of ourselves, we have to examine if there are any flaws in the reasoning HD gave for its position. Remember what HD's basic argument was:

1) Human beings, including their thoughts and feelings and actions, are always determined.
2) Free will is incompatible with determinism.
3) Therefore, human beings are never free.

So if we want to avoid (3), which is the thesis of HD, we need to see if something went wrong in their argument for that position. And here we face two choices. We can try to find a way to deny (1), and argue that we are not in fact determined. That, as we'll see, is the strategy the position known as Libertarianism attempts. But we can also revisit (2), namely the definition of "free will". Perhaps we were too hasty when we agreed that to be free requires that we have open possibility of choice. Perhaps that is the wrong definition of "free will." And perhaps if we redefine what "free will" means, we will hit upon a definition that does leave room for us to be free, at least sometimes. That would be a huge victory it seems, as it would restore some of our sense that we are at least sometimes free. Maybe not always, but at least sometimes. The strategy of redefining "free will"—that is, trying to show that (2) is false, is going to be the essence of the position known as Soft Determinism (SD), or what is also known sometimes as *compatibilism*.

So what does this alternative definition of "free" look like? Why should we think there was something wrong in thinking that to be free requires having the open possibility of choice, as HD insists? Well, perhaps we need to think about a different arena where we make judgments about when someone has acted freely and when they have not.

Think about how criminal courts approach the issue of guilt and responsibility. Suppose you have been accused of committing a crime, and there is no doubt that you are the person who actually did the crime. Is there still a way you might be viewed as not responsible for that action, even though you did it? Think of some of the ways people have tried to prove they were not responsible for actions that they did. Suppose you committed the crime, but only because someone had a gun to your head? Or was threatening your family. Or suppose you stole a loaf of bread, but you were suffering from kleptomania. Or that you were insane or perhaps completely under the control of someone who brainwashed you. Can't we imagine at least some of these cases being ones where we'd say something like "The person did the action, but they can't be blamed for it, because they didn't do the action freely."?

If we can imagine denying in some of these cases that someone acted freely, it must be because we have some standard or definition of what free action looks like, and that in some of these cases the person failed to meet that standard or definition. Here's a proposal for what we might have in mind, in these courtroom cases, when we talk about which actions were done freely:

Courtroom Free Will: An action is free as long as it was not constrained by external forces or compelled by mental illness.

Here, on what we called "Courtroom Free Will," an action has to be free of outside forces, such as threats, and can't be the result of some internal force such as kleptomania or other mental illnesses.

Notice that what we called "Courtroom Free Will" is actually an understanding of what freedom involves that we use in ordinary language and in everyday life. That's part of what goes into deciding whether someone should be held accountable for their actions—namely, whether those actions were done freely. In other words, what we see here is that perhaps, all along, we ourselves operate with this understanding of what it is to be free. That is, and this is the crucial point, there is no mention in any of this of what we saw above under the heading of "incompatibilist" definitions of free will. There is no mention of open possibilities of choice at all. Instead, what we focus on is what *kind of cause* there was for an action. If an action was caused by something external to the person acting (the agent), such as their hand being grabbed, or by something internal like a mental illness, then we think of the action as not free. Otherwise it is considered free.

The point of all of this, remember, is that we were trying to find a way to undermine HD by finding reasons to doubt their definition of "free." And it seems we've done it. For to the extent that we operate with what we initially called "Courtroom Free Will," it seems that that is the better definition of "free."

What about the question of determinism? Well, what is interesting about the position we are developing here, Soft Determinism (SD), is that we can still keep our scientific understanding of human beings as part of the physical world and as therefore determined. But we've seen that whether we are determined is completely irrelevant. What we've focused on, instead, is the definition of "free," and we've found one that seems perfectly compatible with our being determined. That is, we can be free and determined, according to this position.

How is that possible? you might ask. Well there's only a conflict if you think that being free requires open possibility of choice and that humans are in fact determined. The conflict arises only when we define "free" as HD does. But we've now seen that we don't have to, and that in fact, perhaps the better definition of being free is the one which speaks of a lack of internal compulsions, etc. That definition is what we called "Courtroom Free Will" and the idea is that that is the better definition of "free will" than what HD offers. What's crucial for this view, SD, is that we can be free and also determined. In fact, we might see it as a good thing that we are determined. For that just means that our actions are caused, and aren't just happening randomly. So our actions are caused, and thus are determined. But we can still be free, so long as the kind of cause of our action was the right type, namely, something like a wish or desire of ours, but not one that was the result of mental illness or external constraints (just as spelled out in our alternative to HD's definition of "free").

This, admittedly, is a difficult position to wrap your head around. The key is to remember that we can be free and determined because "free" only means the action wasn't externally constrained or compelled. As a colleague puts it: "Soft Determinism" is soft on "freedom"; meaning that it doesn't require something difficult to achieve, such as open possibility of choice. In that way it is "soft." But it is still a version of determinism, just like HD.

The following chart might help, and will pave the way for our third position, Libertarianism.

	Incompatibilist?	Always Determined?	Ever Free?
Hard Determinism	Yes	Yes	No
Soft Determinism	No	Yes	Yes
Libertarianism	Yes	No	Yes

Courtesy Eric Rubenstein.

Libertarianism

We've seen one way to resist HD's pessimistic conclusion that we are never free, and that was SD's attempt to find a better definition of "free will," one that is easier to satisfy. There is a third position, however, which we will explore now. Part of the challenge of SD, that we just reviewed, is convincing ourselves that it can be possible to be determined and still free. That, as we saw, requires us to think of the definition of "free" as not requiring genuine alternative choices, but as simply the absence of certain kinds of forces causing us to act. It is not unreasonable, however, to ask of SD: Yes, perhaps I'm free in the sense of not being compelled to act, but am I *really* free? where one is wondering if it would have been possible to have chosen differently. Because SD is a version of determinism, it is going to deny that in that particular situation it would have been possible to choose from more than one possible alternative.

That is, looking at our chart, it may be hard to shake the feelings that HD's definition of "free" is correct, what we called the "incompatibilist" definition. But if we take that as our definition of what being free involves, we have to worry about the apparent fact that we are determined in everything we do. Putting those two beliefs together is what yields the problematic HD conclusion that free will is just an illusion. But maybe there is another way. Maybe we can say that being free *does* require there to be open possibilities for choice, just as HD says, *but* then to continue on by saying that in fact, we humans *are* capable of making such free choices. That is, perhaps we can try to argue that we do in fact have the ability, in one and the same situation, to choose from multiple avenues of action. That is to say, perhaps we in fact are not always determined.

This is the position of Libertarianism (L), namely that sometimes human beings really have open possibilities available to them. The appeal of this view is that it finds a way to restore our belief that we are sometimes, at least, truly free, and it does so without resorting to a new definition of free, as SD does.

In this way Libertarianism (L) is a very appealing position. The challenge, however, is to see if we can truly make sense of it, once we start to think through what it is really saying. Imagine, then, that you are in the mood to smoke a cigar. You've got a desire to do so and there is one in front of you. To be free, according to L, it has to be that whatever it is you end up doing, smoking the cigar or not, that you could have also done the opposite—that there really were at least two alternate possibilities available for you. So let us say that you did smoke the cigar. We don't want to say, if we are defending L, that you were caused to do it by things like your genetics and desires and habits. Why not? Because, as we've seen, those are all the kinds of causes that are deterministic causes—and thus ones that wouldn't allow for the possibility that you could have done something other than what you were (determined) to do.

But, and this is important, we don't want to say that your action of smoking was just random either. Why not? Because random actions aren't truly yours. If you truly did something randomly there's no reason to give you credit or blame for it, as there's an important sense in which you didn't do it. It just happened. There was no reason or explanation for why it happened—as that is what it means to say that something happened randomly. So, your smoking the cigar has to be an action that was not determined but also not random. Did your smoking the cigar have a cause? Well, yes, it has to, otherwise it would be just a random occurrence. But if it is caused, doesn't that make it like all the causes we've been talking about—one cause leading to one and only one effect?

In other words, if it is caused in the way we usually speak of causes, then it is seems to have to be a deterministic cause, which is to send us back to HD. What we need, it seems, is a cause that is a *non-determining cause*. Advocates of Libertarianism sometimes even give this kind of cause a name, calling it "agent causation" which means that the cause of the action was just the person. They caused it to happen, but they weren't determined in their bringing it about, as they could have, supposedly, done something completely different.

The debate here can get pretty complicated, so we'll leave the position of Libertarianism with just this one question: Can you make sense of a cause that is a non-deterministic cause? If you can, then perhaps L is a viable theory. If you cannot, then we are forced to go back to either SD or HD. A related issue is this. According to L, you caused the action in question. And that cause was allegedly a non-determining cause. You yourself brought it about that you smoked the cigar, say. But, crucially, it also has to be that nothing in you caused you to smoke the cigar. That is, you caused it to be smoked, but when we go back a step in the chain of causes and effects, it can't be that something like a nicotine-addiction caused you to pick up the cigar. For that again would be a determining cause.

So the cause of the action had to be you, but nothing could have caused you to cause the action. So where did your cause of the action come from? We're used to thinking of there being a continuous line of causes and effects. Only now we seem to have to accept a break in that chain: various things happen around you that cause other things, and which cause you to have experiences, but the chain ends when it comes to your (free) actions, as nothing about you, your genetics or character could be the cause of you picking up and smoking the cigar. Nothing could have caused you to smoke it, or we would be right back where we started—a determining cause, one which would, combined with our incompatibilist definition of free, would lead us to say the action wasn't free at all. And that, again, seems to make it quite mysterious how we manage to do anything free, no matter what L insists.

As we've seen, the debate over free will is a complex one, involving lots of twists and turns. Before we can hope to decide which position is the best one, we have to make sure that we understand what each one says. Arguably the hardest part of defending the last position, L, is that it is difficult to find the right words to explain how exactly it works.

All of that said, as we go forward, and as you think about other philosophical topics, you might want to keep an eye open for how many of them actually assume that we are free. And now you know that that assumption is far from being an easy one to defend. Sometimes, in other words, in philosophy, we might make progress by recognizing where there are problems and puzzles that we still have to find a solution to.

CHAPTER 6

Ethics

Competing Intuitions about Morality

In this chapter we turn to a major area of philosophy: ethics. Philosophers who study ethics or morality (we'll use those words interchangeably) find themselves with lots of different questions, including ones about why people are motivated to do what they do, why we sometimes do things that we know are bad for ourselves and others; whether there are ultimate, objective truths about what is right or wrong, or whether what is right is merely relative to a given culture; whether morality depends on religion. A full book on ethics would be needed to address all of the questions that arise. We will focus here on one small but central question: What makes right actions right in the first place? That is, if something is the right thing to do, what factors or aspects are responsible for making it the right thing to do? (And if it is the wrong action, what makes it wrong?)

We all know that we ought to do the right thing. But figuring out what the right thing to do in a given situation is often difficult. In this chapter we will examine two famous accounts of what makes right actions right, and thus will have two theories which can be applied to situations where we are trying to figure out what the right thing to do is.

The interesting twist in this chapter is that though the two theories we will examine are incompatible, you will likely find yourself sympathetic at times to each of them. In fact, each of the two philosophers we'll examine, Mill and Kant, claimed that they were simply taking our common-sense views of morality and making them more explicit and clear, giving details and justifications for things we already believe. If this is correct—that Mill and Kant are both simply giving voice to what we already think makes right actions right, and if indeed these two views are truly incompatible, that means that each of us walks around with conflicting viewpoints about how to act. That can be at least one explanation for why we sometimes find it hard to know how to act in certain situations, because we at root have competing intuitions driving our decision-making process.

As such, a central aim of this chapter is to explore each of these two theories, with the goal of having you decide which you think is the better one. Now the two philosophers we'll be discussing have radically different views about why some things are the right thing to do and some things are wrong. Before we get to their views, we'll see what I mean about how we already have within ourselves an inchoate understanding of these theories—that we already operate with them, just not in the fully explicit and clear way that comes from philosophical reflection on those theories. To do this we'll work through an example of a moral problem, one that very well may trigger sympathy for both of these two moral theories. This in turn will prove a helpful starting place as we begin the process of thinking more clearly and thoroughly about why certain actions are right/wrong.

Consider this example. You are dating someone here at college. Over Spring Break you see someone you used to date. You are thrilled to see each other again, and end up being unfaithful to the person you are dating at college. (Side note: there are lots of ways of being unfaithful, so it doesn't have to mean sex that we're talking about.) Now the question that confronts you, when the person you are dating here at school asks why you are acting so odd lately, is: Do you tell them the truth about your infidelity, or do you lie?

Now the first thing you should do for this exercise is think about *what* you would do. Would you tell them the truth? Would you lie? But even more importantly, as this exercise is intended to serve a philosophical purpose, and as we've seen, philosophers care about reasons for our beliefs, you should ask *why* one option seems like the right thing to do. Why is one action better than the other? (We're assuming here you are trying to do the right thing, and are genuinely wrestling with the right thing to do is). Think about those two questions: *What* would you do? *Why* should you do it?

As we'll see, it is the *why* that really matters here, as that is key to understanding the different moral philosophies at work. Depending on the details of the situation, one moral theory could have you acting in one way under some circumstances and a different way under the other. That's why I want you to focus more on *why* you would act a certain way, and not just on what you would do.

As you think through this example (and here I recommend you put the book down for a moment or two and genuinely think through the example), I suspect one line of thinking you'll find yourself with is this. "Well, if I tell the truth I'll hurt this person I care about. And they will definitely be angry with me. And they might even break up with me. That would make both of us unhappy. So I will lie, to avoid this unhappiness." Or you might find yourself thinking, "Well, if I lie and say that nothing happened when I saw my 'ex,' the person here at college might find out from one of their friends. And if I get caught in a lie then they will really be mad at me, and will likely break up with me. That will cause us both pain, and so I should tell the truth."

Now notice that in the above paragraph we found ourselves with different courses of action—first we found a reason to lie, and then we found a reason to tell the truth. But when we go deeper, and ask why we were going to do one action or the other, we find that both answers are actually driven by the same thing. What is that? Well, in both scenarios we are trying to avoid pain and unhappiness. Our decision to lie or tell the truth in this example is based simply on our best estimation of which course of action will cause the least amount of pain—and depending on the facts of the situation— who you are dating, how long, whether you had promised to see only each other—you might get a different action. But, again, what is driving your decision is really a concern to avoid unhappiness. In other words, in this situation you are thinking about the *consequences* of your action, and thinking about which action will produce the greatest amount of happiness (or, to the same point, at least the smallest amount of pain).

This view—that what matters is the consequences, where it is the consequences which determine what the right thing to do is—is going to be the first theory we explore. It has been developed by different philosophers over the centuries, and we're going to look at the version that comes from the philosopher John Stuart Mill. The name for this theory—the one which focuses on consequences—is *Utilitarianism*.

Now even if you found yourself thinking about which course of action will cause the least amount of pain/the greatest amount of happiness, I bet there's another way of thinking you also found yourself with. It might go something like this: "I've been dating this person at college for several months. We really like each other. And we trust each other. I shouldn't have cheated on them, and now I'm faced with how to deal with it. I ought to do the right thing. What I owe them, as part of the trust we established, is to tell them the truth. I really am obligated to tell them the truth, even though it may cause us both unhappiness. Even though it may cause our relationship to end, I have a duty or obligation to tell them the truth. They deserve the truth, after all."

Now if you found yourself thinking along those lines you are doing something that goes exactly against the direction of the Utilitarianism we first mentioned. For instead of thinking about the consequences, you are thinking about what your duties or obligations are. And in reflecting on the fact that you care about this person, you realize you have certain duties to them, including the duty to tell the truth to them, no matter the consequences. This way of looking at things is the first steps toward a theory of right/wrong known as "deontology" (which comes from the Greek word for "duty"). As an ethical theory it was most famously developed by the German philosopher, Immanuel Kant. We'll explore that theory as well.

Notice what I said before about these theories being incompatible—that you can't combine them. We can see clearly already why not. For one of them looks to the consequences to see what the right thing to do is, while the other says consequences aren't what matter. They are looking, in other words, at completely different things in their assessment of what the right thing to do is.

So now that you've gotten a little hint of how the two theories work, we'll go through them more thoroughly, with the aim of understanding how each one works in detail. Once we've done that for both, you'll be in a better position to decide which theory you think is better. And that will give you an enriched understanding of how you should choose to act when faced with your own moral dilemmas.

Utilitarianism

We'll begin by looking at things from a very high level of abstraction. Doing so will offer us yet another way to see the difference between Utilitarianism and Deontology, a deeper way. Think back to your deliberations about which action would minimize pain. When you were thinking about how to avoid causing pain it was because you thought of pain as a bad thing. And so you were trying to avoid that which is bad. The right action, in other words, was that which minimized the bad stuff (pain), or put differently, maximized the good stuff—pleasure or happiness. As a philosophical way of putting this, we can say that when it comes to Utilitarianism, what is good/bad is prior to what is right/wrong. By "prior" we don't mean what is first, but rather what is most basic. And this theory says what is most basic is what is good (pleasure) and the right thing to do tries to maximize that which is good. What the right thing to do is, in other words, dependent upon an answer to a more basic question, namely, what is good? The good is prior to the right, says the Utilitarian. (When we get to Kant, we'll see just the opposite—that the right is prior to the good. That will be a little harder to understand, but right now you can see how this shows in yet another way why the two theories are incompatible—that what is most basic differs for each.)

In our discussions so far we've also hit upon some additional, important points about Utilitarianism. Let us make them explicit now. We can say, first, that Utilitarianism focuses on the consequences of our actions. But which consequences are the ones that matter? The ones that have to do with happiness. So, we can say that Utilitarianism is:

a) Consequentialist: It bases what is right/wrong on the consequences of what we do.
b) Hedonistic: What is good/bad is happiness/unhappiness.

A word about (b) is in order. To say Utilitarianism is hedonistic is just to say that among the many consequences of our actions, the ones that matter are the ones that influence how much happiness or unhappiness there is, for Utilitarianism holds pleasure/happiness as what is truly valuable.

What is happiness? Well, that itself is an important philosophical question in its own right. But for now we'll say that happiness is pleasure, unhappiness is pain. And in saying that what we really care about is increasing pleasure (or minimizing pain), we are saying that what is valuable or good is pleasure. That is all we mean by "hedonistic"—that pleasure is valued. We are going to ignore the connotations that sometimes come with the word "hedonism"— namely that someone who is a hedonist cares about only crude bodily pleasures, by simply acknowledging that there are lots of different kinds of pleasures: the pleasure of friendship, the pleasure of having a stimulating conversation, and also the pleasure of having an ice cream cone. Those are all pleasurable experiences, and we can say that they are all different kinds of pleasures. There's not just one, there are many kinds of pleasures. The Utilitarian cares about creating the greatest amount of pleasure, whatever kinds they may be.

Now we've seen that Utilitarians care about maximizing that which is good—i.e., pleasure, we can ask about *whose* pleasure matters. Is it just the person acting (the "agent")? Is it only the people the agent cares about? The answer to both of these is "no," and the pleasure that matters is that of everyone who is affected by an action. Importantly, though different people may experience different amounts of pain or pleasure, each person's pain and pleasure matters equally. Your pleasure, that is, when you act, is no more nor no less important than the pleasure of others. Everyone counts equally we may say, and that gives us our third main point about Utilitarianism. We'll put it as saying that Utilitarianism is "egalitarian" in that everyone's pleasure/pain is just as important as everyone else's. So, in review, we have the three main tenets of Utilitarianism. The theory is:

a) Consequentialist: It bases what is right/wrong on the consequences of what we do.
b) Hedonistic: It thinks what is valuable is happiness, understood as pleasure.
c) Egalitarian: Everyone's pleasure or pain is just as important as another person's.

Put simply, Utilitarianism says that the morally correct thing to do is to maximize pleasure, where we can imagine comparing different courses of action, and picking the one that creates the greatest amount of pleasure in total. (Here you should imagine that we can assign units of measure for pain and pleasure, and then proceed by calculating the total amount of happiness, where you take each possible course of action, consider who will be affected and how much pleasure or pain each person will get, adding up the units of pleasure while subtracting the units of pain, and arriving at a net sum for each course of action. The right way to proceed will be to follow the path that creates the greatest amount of happiness, once everyone who is affected is taken into consideration.)

Note, we're not seeking to make the greatest amount of people happy. It is happiness itself we are seeking to maximize, however it is distributed. Why? Because, recall, we had decided that happiness is what is ultimately good. So, faced with the option of creating a world with more good stuff in it versus a world with less of that good stuff, the Utilitarian thinks the obvious thing to do is to bring about that world with the greatest amount of good stuff, i.e., pleasure.

Now an important thing to realize here is that the right action, that which maximizes happiness compared with other available actions, may very well depend on the circumstances, where one and the same action that is the right thing to do in one situation is exactly the wrong thing to do in another. Consider the act of stealing a loaf of bread versus not stealing it. If the circumstances were such that stealing the loaf of bread were to feed oneself when starving, and stealing it from a multimillionaire that very well might be the right thing to do in that situation. But if one were to steal the loaf of bread just to get the thrill of shoplifting, and if it were stolen from a store that was struggling to survive, that act of stealing might be the wrong thing to do as it doesn't maximize happiness.[2]

---

[2] The position we are discussing here is officially known as "Act Utilitarianism," and contrasts with what is called "Rule Utilitarianism." The latter is beyond the scope of this book.

Deontology

Let us return to the example we started with. We've seen that one way you might decide how to act would involve thinking through your options and picking the course of action which would maximize happiness (or, at least, minimize unhappiness). But we also saw that there is a different way to think about your choice. Instead of thinking about the consequences, you might think about what duties you have to someone you are in a relationship with, what those duties require you to do, and why you have those duties in the first place. That, we saw, is the path taken by Kant, and we will elaborate his theory, Deontology, here.

Let us begin by noticing something we've not talked at all about so far. (Sometimes what people don't say can be as important as what they do.) We've not talked at all about the importance of why someone has acted in a certain way. We've not spoken of their motives, that is. Usually, though, we do think a person's motives for acting are relevant in deciding whether they have done something good or bad, right or wrong. A person who tells the truth only to avoid the pain involved in later getting caught in a lie is likely to be viewed differently than someone who feels an obligation to tell the truth out of respect for the person s/he loves.

For Kant, the best kind of action—the way of acting that earns our greatest respect, and the one that we should all aim for doing—involves not just doing the right thing, but doing it for the proper reason (i.e., the proper motive). Kant, in fact, thinks that when you have done the right action (your duty) for the right reason that you've done something so special and good that it is good regardless of the consequences, and good regardless of the conditions or circumstances. The phrase he uses for someone's doing the right thing for the right reason is that they have acted with a "good will." A good will, Kant thinks, is the highest of all goods. To appreciate Kant who believes a good will is so good requires we understand several things, including what the right action is (what our duties are) and also what the best kind of motive for action there is. Let us start with the second—motives for acting.

To make things simpler, and so that we don't have too many questions and debates going on at the same time, let us assume for the sake of argument that telling the truth in the example we're using is the right thing to do. Let us assume, that is, that we have a duty to tell the truth to a loved one. Even still, just because you've told the truth to someone (and thus done your duty) doesn't mean you've acted with a good will. Why not? Because it depends on why you told the truth, what your motives were.

Kant thinks there are three different kinds of motives for our acting, and only one of them is the special kind—where we act with what he called a good will. In our example, you might have told the truth (and thus done your duty) but only for selfish or ulterior motives, say because you wanted to seem like a good person, or because you wanted to alleviate your own guilt. It is still good that you told the truth, but if you found out that that was why someone told you that truth about their being unfaithful—that they did it just to get rid of their own guilt—you wouldn't think they've acted in a particularly commendable way. They don't deserve to be praised for that action, given why they told the truth. So, in general, one motive for doing our duty is out of selfish or ulterior motives, which we've seen is hardly the best kind of motive.

The second kind of motive is where we do the right thing (our duty) because we have positive feelings or desires at work. We tell the truth, that is, because we want the other person to know the truth, or because we care about them. Now that might seem like an ideal situation—you told the truth and did it because you care about the person (even though you did cheat on them). We'll soon see why Kant thinks that's still not good enough to count as acting with a good will.

The third kind of motive for acting is a bit different, and harder to appreciate at first. Sometimes, Kant says, we do the right thing because we know it is the right thing to do. We contemplate what we should do, and we do the right thing because we know we have a duty to do that action. In this example, you would tell the truth because you recognize you have a duty to tell the truth. And that recognition of your duty is what motivated you to tell the truth—not because you wanted to make yourself feel better, or even out of concern or feeling for the other person, but simply because you recognized you had to tell the truth, and that motivated you to do it—it was the reason you told the truth, even though it was hard and even though it might cause bad consequences.

According to Kant, this last type of motive is the best kind: you do your duty because you appreciate that it is your duty. You are motivated by your recognition that you have to tell the truth. That is what counts as acting with a good will. But why is it so special? Why is it better than the others, especially the second type, where you are acting out of a concern for someone else, where you are guided by your feelings? Why isn't that good enough?

Here we get to the heart of Kant's philosophy. Kant thinks that human beings can be motivated by two different kinds of forces: feelings or desires, on the one hand, and reason, on the other. By reason he means something like our ability to recognize what is required of us, and our thinking it through that we ought to act a certain way. For Kant, it is better to be motivated by reason than it is to be motivated by feelings. That's why the good will involves doing your duty because you recognize it is your duty—you've used your reasoning powers. But, still, what is so good about that, and why isn't being motivated by feelings, including feelings of love and concern, and a desire to help others, good enough for Kant?

That is a key question, and exactly where Kant and other philosophers may part company and disagree with each other. For Kant, we should be guided by reason and not by feelings. Why? Kant himself has different answers, but the most important one, I think, is that feelings and desires are not things we have control over. The world (and our bodies) cause us to have different feelings and desires, and we don't have much say over what we happen to be feeling or wanting at a given moment. Yes, we can control whether we act on our desires or feelings, but we don't have much control over them.

So imagine that the reason you acted was because you had certain feelings or desires. When we realize that those feelings or desires were not things we had much control over, then it seems that our acting was caused by forces we didn't have much control over. And that means there is an important sense in which it wasn't *our* action at all. We were just pushed and pulled in different directions, just like an animal that acts because of whatever desire it has at the moment is strongest. We don't in other words, seem to be acting truly freely, and our actions aren't truly our own if we don't have control over them. And we don't have complete control over them if what motivated or caused us to act were those feelings or desires. (If it helps, think back to our discussions of free will: we don't seem to be acting freely if we're caused to act by forces we don't have control over.)

On the other hand, Kant thinks we do have control over our reason. We can choose how we think about something, we have control over what we decide to believe, etc. And thus when we are motivated by reason then we are truly in control of that action. We have what Kant calls "autonomy"—we are in complete control of what we are doing, and are deciding to ignore our feelings and desires, and instead do that which we recognize is the right thing to do. When that happens our actions are truly our own. And that is what we want— to be the true cause of our actions, instead of being pushed and pulled by our desires the way animals are. Thus, finally, we can see why Kant thinks the best motive for action is the recognition—by your faculty of reason—that you have a duty to tell the truth. When that is what leads you to act, then you have acted with a good will.

As I said, when you act with a good will, you've done something truly special. Also, something that is hard to do, as it isn't easy to ignore your desires and do what you know you have to do. Sometimes we can even feel the tug of war inside ourselves—our desires pulling us one way, while our recognition that we should act differently pulls us in the opposite direction. When reason wins, we've done something special and difficult—and special because it is difficult. In fact, it is so good that it doesn't even matter what the consequences are. So long as you do your duty for the reason it is your duty, you've done something truly special, even if the consequences turn out bad.

What Are Our Duties?

So far we've only addressed Kant's views about the kinds of things that can motivate us to act. We've still not addressed, though, how we should act and what we ought to be doing. We've not said, in other words, anything about what our duties actually are.

Kant's way of articulating our duties is by speaking of what he calls the "categorical imperative" (CI). The CI tells us what we have to do. An imperative is a command; and by "categorical" Kant means a command that is universal with no exceptions. Kant thinks this is how the rules of morality work: they tell us how we have to behave, and that we always have to behave that way. There is no time when we're free to do whatever we want. The rules of morality are always in force, which is perhaps why it is hard to be a good person sometimes, as we never get a "day off."

What then is it that we always have to do? Kant himself gives three different formulations or expressions of the CI. We'll focus on the second, what he calls the "Humanity Formulation of the Categorical Imperative." It says, "Always treat the humanity in yourself and others never merely as a means but always as an end." Now there is a lot packed into that, so let us pull the pieces apart to really appreciate what Kant is saying.

"Humanity" is the key notion for Kant, and by it he doesn't mean a biological category, such as the species of human. Instead he is referring to our rational capacities. Reason, as we've seen repeatedly, is at the heart of Kant's philosophy. But in this context Kant means by rational capacity not only our ability to do philosophy or mathematics, but something more practical, namely our ability to set goals for ourselves. This can include short-term goals or ends, or long-term major ones, such as what we want to do with our lives. This ability to plan, set goals or ends, is critical in distinguishing us from other beings. Interestingly, we need not hold that humanity (i.e., rational capacities) means all and only human beings. For on the one hand we can imagine humans (in the biological sense) not able to engage in such planning (such as infants), and in the other direction we can imagine non-humans who can think and make plans or set goals (with a little imagination we might picture aliens, or perhaps beings closer to home, say if we discover that some chimps or whales or dolphins have much greater cognitive capacities that we haven't realized.)

The point here is that such special capacities are deserving of respect and special treatment. The essence of such treatment, in Kant's eyes, is to not treat beings who have such capacities as if they were mere objects. Think of the paradigm of how humans have mistreated one another, such as in having slaves. Kant's philosophy has a plausible way of explaining what is terrible about slavery, namely that it treats human beings who have the capacity to plan and craft their own lives as if they were mere objects. What's more, slaves were treated as a mere means to other's happiness, such as economic benefit. And that brings us to the next point, Kant's talk of "mere means."

We all have to use each other, in some sense, because none of us are fully self-sufficient. We depend on others to educate us, or grow food for us, or to make our clothing. And typically there is nothing wrong with benefiting from or using other people's skills. But there is always a limit to how we can use people. We can't go so far as to treat them as mere objects, neglecting or forgetting that they have their own goals and ends. That is what Kant is getting at in talking of treating others as ends—namely, that we must always respect these rational capacities wherever they are found. We cannot use people as a means, even if is to produce happiness for all. That, of course, is exactly where Kant differs from Mill. We are not allowed to do whatever it takes to maximize happiness, for there are limits on how we can treat others. That limit is what Kant is getting at in the Humanity Formulation of the categorical imperative.

What would treating someone's humanity with respect look like? Consider the example we've been using, of infidelity. When we lie to another person, or withhold important information, we deprive them of the information they need to be able to use their rational capacities. A person can't make a good plan for themselves if they've been denied pertinent information. The person you've cheated on, for instance, isn't able to make an informed decision about what to do about your infidelity if they are denied the information they need. Put differently, in lying to another about something so important, chances are you would be doing it to maximize happiness (minimize pain), and so in that sense you've used that person as a mere means to achieve your own goals. And that is to treat another as if they were a mere object or tool, used to achieve one's own goal. That is exactly what Kant thinks we can never do. We are always, no matter what, required to refrain from treating another as a mere means. This imperative, the duty we have to always follow, puts limits on how we can act.

We can now return to the abstract point we began our discussions with. With Kant in mind, think about what would happen if we use another as a mere means to help us accomplish a goal we have. We've done something wrong, Kant thinks. Here's the extra point, namely that the thing we've accomplished is no longer a good thing, even if it is something we thought was what we wanted. In other words, the supposed happiness we've brought about by treating another as an object is tarnished. By using immoral means to achieve an end we have, that end is no longer even a good thing. In those abstract terms we used before, the right is now prior to the good. That is, what is moral or right sets limits on what is good. This is exactly the opposite of what we saw with Utilitarianism.

Think back now to that point about Utilitarianism, and how it says that the good is more basic or prior to the right. That is, again, the right action depends on something more basic, namely what is good, i.e., pleasure, and so to act in the right way requires we bring about that which is more fundamental—pleasure or happiness.

Kant, as we've seen, has the opposite view. Namely, he thinks the right is prior to the good. What does that mean? We know that we always have to respect the rational capacities of ourselves and others. That is basic and fundamental. In fact, it is so basic and fundamental, that if we fail to act according to the Categorical Imperative (CI), we negate any good consequences. That is, what is good depends on our doing the right thing. To make this less abstract, think about a situation where you've maximized happiness, but did it by torturing, humiliating, or at worst, enslaving someone. Yes, you might have created more happiness by lying or humiliating someone. But if you acted that way, you've broken the CI, and thus you've ruined the good consequences it seems. In our example, suppose you bring about the greatest amount of happiness by lying to the person you love about your infidelity. In that case you've used them as a mere means to bring about happiness. You've not given them the truth, and so deprived them of the information they need to decide how to act—whether to forgive you or break up with you, for example. And in denying them that information, you've brought about happiness, yes, but at the price of not respecting the other person. And so that happiness isn't actually good, as it was brought about by immoral means.

That, in fact, is an easy way to see the difference between Utilitarianism and Deontology: Do the ends justify the means? Let's suppose the ends are happiness for all. Does a Utilitarian think we can do anything we need to to attain those ends, that happiness? Yes, because what is good—happiness—is what is most important. Anything it takes to maximize happiness is legitimate. What about for Kant? No. You can't achieve happiness by humiliating others or disrespecting them or treating them as objects. The ends don't let us do whatever it takes to get to them. And if we end up not respecting the rational capacities of others (and ourselves), then any happiness we do achieve has been tainted. In more abstract terms again: the right is more basic than the good. How we treat others determines whether we've done something good or not.

CHAPTER 7

Suicide

Duties to Others and One's Own Self

Suicide is a difficult subject to talk about. It is both a highly charged moral issue as well as an emotional one. Coupled with traditional religious views about its permissibility, it can be hard to think clearly about suicide. That makes it all the more appropriate for a philosophical investigation, one that permits one to think clearly about a difficult topic. In this chapter we'll outline some of the arguments used to try and prove that suicide is immoral, and then see if those arguments withstand scrutiny. Much of what we'll discuss is covered in a famous essay by the eighteenth-century Scottish philosopher, David Hume.

In an earlier chapter we've looked at different accounts of right/wrong. We might begin by briefly applying those theories to the issue of suicide and see what we can uncover about whether it is immoral or not. Consider how a utilitarian might approach the subject. Here, as we saw, the rightness or wrongness of the action will depend on the circumstances, namely, those where committing suicide would create greater happiness on the whole than not. We would, as Utilitarians do, look to the consequences of the act of suicide.

If we remember that Utilitarians think that the minimization of pain is the flip side of the same coin as increasing happiness, we can think about the potential reduction of pain for the person suffering who commits suicide. That, of course, would have to be factored alongside the predictable pain that is likely to come to friends and family of the person who commits suicide. Making this especially complicated is that we'd have to weigh the reduction of suffering for the person who commits suicide against the potential happiness that might someday come to the person who is presently suffering. Not knowing what the future holds for anyone can make it hard to assess whether suicide would maximize happiness for the person contemplating it.

Perhaps there are clear cases, however, where we can speak to whether suicide would maximize happiness for the person contemplating (remembering that happiness/unhappiness would have to be factored in alongside that of everyone else who would be affected by the person's suicide). Consider, for example, cases, where someone is suffering from a terrible and terminal illness, who is suffering greatly with little to no hope for improvement. In such cases I think we can imagine that suicide might bring relief to the suffering person, and perhaps even to those who care about that person. But as we've said, it would depend on the circumstances. If anything, though, those are the easiest of cases—where a person is suffering from a terminal illness. There are other, much more complicated cases we should consider as well.

Before doing that, let us briefly reintroduce Kant's account of morality into the discussion. Kant, as we saw, thinks it is always wrong to treat the humanity (i.e., one's rational capacities) of any being as a mere means. Kant himself thought suicide always wrong, for he thought it involved a violation of a duty we have to ourselves, namely to not use our humanity as a mere mean to achieve a goal, where in this case the goal would be remove suffering. So even in the most dire of cases, such as in terminal illness, Kant thinks suicide is wrong. This contrasts with the Utilitarian who holds the door open where at least some situations would make it morally permissible.

This brings us to a central question: Does suicide violate a duty we have to ourselves? We've seen, briefly, how our two moral theories might approach that question. We started with the easier cases (not that any are truly easy, but relatively so), namely where we are considering the suicide of someone suffering from a terminal illness. (This debate is related to another, one about the morality of euthanasia, which we will not have an opportunity to explore in this book.) A harder case to think about would be where someone is contemplating suicide because they are depressed. Can suicide ever be a rational and moral thing to do for someone who is in that state of extreme depression?

This is an important but difficult question itself, one that brings other disciplines into the discussion besides philosophy, such as psychology and sociology, to name two. Many people think that anyone who is suicidal has to be irrational, as no rational person would want to take their own life. Here, though, we have to be careful, as we don't want to assume that suicide is automatically irrational: the cases of terminal illness above show how it might not be irrational.

But for the person who is suicidal from depression, things can be much harder to assess, particularly for the depressed person. Many people who at one point were suicidally depressed but later had their depression lifted, look back and think it would have been a mistake and the wrong thing to do to have committed suicide when they were depressed. Depression, after all, can make it hard to think clearly about anything, particularly about one's own future. And that makes it extremely difficult to answer the question we asked: namely, does suicide involve a violation of a duty one has to one's self?

Perhaps we'd need to look more closely at such questions as whether a suicidal person has already lost some of their cognitive capacities, which would make it unclear whether they were in fact using their humanity merely as a means. And is it fair to ask a suicidal person to continue suffering (as depression can be every bit as painful as other diseases or ailments) because it would (as Kant thinks) treat one's humanity merely as a means to removing that suffering? Isn't it cruel to demand of someone that they continue suffering? Or, alternatively, perhaps we do have such a strong duty to respect our humanity that we are never allowed to throw one's life away, as Kant put it, simply to reduce suffering. We're not allowed to kill others, it seems, to minimize suffering. Why should it matter if the person suffering is the same person who is considering suicide?

So far, then, we've seen immediately how difficult the subject can be to think clearly about. But let us continue with other reasons people have given for thinking it is immoral, including, in general, the view that suicide violates a duty we have to others, and finally, that it somehow violates a duty we may have to God. Here our discussion will be less explicitly connected with Kant's and Mill's theories, though they will figure in the background (as perhaps will our earlier discussions about death itself).

On the question of whether suicide is wrong because it violates a duty we have to others, we can think of a common expression used—that suicide is the "ultimate selfish action." When people say that it is presumably because they think that the person who has committed (or considered) suicide is thinking only of their own pain and suffering, and not those who may love or care about them. Let us put it directly, though: Would you demand of someone who is suffering from depression, that they continue to stay alive in order to not cause *you* harm? Is that a fair burden to put on another person, if they are truly suffering? Why do they have such a strong duty to you? Or, put differently, are you placing a reasonable demand on another to ask that they continue to suffer? In fact, one might even turn the argument around by making the case that if you do care about someone who is suffering that you would want their suffering to end, wouldn't you? If that is right, then doesn't it make suicide perhaps acceptable in some cases?

Here we may find ourselves having to revisit an earlier consideration. For often people say to the suicidally depressed person things like, "You don't know what the future holds; you very well could get rid of the depression someday." That is, we might find ourselves returning to the question of whether people owe it to themselves to stay alive, even if they are suffering, because someday their depression may be healed. To that, of course, we would have to ask, among other things, questions about how much suffering a person should be asked to endure, and when enough is enough.

These are all difficult but important questions. Let us turn now, however, to a completely different consideration that many have given for why suicide is wrong. Many have argued that suicide is immoral because it somehow violates a duty we have to God, or, relatedly, that it is disruptive to God's plan, or is somehow unnatural. That is a pretty commonly expressed reason for thinking suicide is wrong, and so we should look more carefully and thoroughly at it.

Duties to God

Is suicide wrong because it is in some manner an affront to God? Let's examine some of the reasons people have given for thinking suicide is somehow disrespectful to God, or the "divine order," as Hume puts it. Here's we'll briefly state each reason, and then go back and explore each in more detail.

1) Some have argued that suicide is offensive to God because it is disrespectful of the gift of we have received from God.
2) Some have contended that suicide is unnatural, and in that way is offensive to God.
3) Some have argued that suicide violates God's plan for us and the universe.

Regarding (1): Leaving the issue of suicide for the moment, we do tend to think that human life is valuable, even precious. We think of murder as one of the worst crimes that can be committed, of the tragedies of war as humanity's greatest failings, both presumably because we think the destruction of a human is a terrible thing. It is terrible, in other words, to destroy something so significant and valuable as a human life. (Though we won't discuss it here, it is a similar sentiment which is behind what people refer to as "pro-life" views about abortion.)

What's more, for many people, this precious life is something that is given to us by God. If indeed human life is precious and given to us by God then it would seem, at the least, to be disrespectful of that gift of life, and of God in turn, by committing suicide. It is offensive to God because it involves the destruction of something precious, something bestowed upon us by God.

What might we say in response to this? Here Hume has a number of points to make. One is that while we ourselves view human life as precious, from the perspective of the universe as a whole, any individual life is quite insignificant. Compared to the size and age of the universe, humans are no more than dust, or as Hume puts it, human life, from the general point of view of the universe is no more precious or valuable than that of an oyster, something we don't tend to think twice about destroying. What's more, we might note that it is at best ironic that if human life is so valuable that it can be destroyed by something as insignificant as a bacteria or virus. Humans, also, unfortunately, die in horrible ways, ways which might suggest that God doesn't in fact view life as so significant. If human life is indeed not so significant, then the taking of it wouldn't seem to be something offensive to God.

Now in response to that point, one might note that it is still God who decides when we live or when we die, and thus suicide is still wrong because it violates God's plan for us and the universe. We'll return to this point when we look at (3) more closely. For now, as a final point about (1)—that suicide is wrong because it doesn't show the proper respect for the life that God has given, we might consider the following: If God has indeed given us the gift of life, isn't it then ours to do with it as we want? Isn't the very life that we've been given one that includes the power to make decisions? Why can't one be appreciative of the gift of life from God, and also appreciative of the ability that comes with that life, namely, to end it once that life has become too burdensome or difficult? Wouldn't that still be respectful of God? Why, that is, does respecting the gift of life require that we continue to live a life that has become full of pain and misery?

Regarding (2): Thinking about that question can lead us to our second point, (2) from above. That said that suicide is an affront to God because it somehow is unnatural. And so perhaps the reason we might think suicide is wrong is that destroying that life, even when it is full of misery, is somehow unnatural or goes against the "divine order" of how things should be.

Here we run into an issue that is actually quite important, and one that goes well beyond just the discussion of suicide. Many activities that humans engage in have been condemned because they are supposedly "unnatural." To help us decide if that judgment is correct, we have to be clear about what we in fact mean when we say that something is unnatural.

What then do we mean when we say that something is unnatural? We can't just mean that we don't like it, or think that it is wrong, because what we are trying to figure out is whether suicide is in fact wrong. To simply declare it wrong because it is supposedly unnatural, and that "unnatural" just means something we don't like or think is wrong is to argue in a circle. Now here's an interesting twist on the word "unnatural," namely, that anything which happens in nature is natural—"natural" just means what happens in nature. If that is right, then nothing actually could be unnatural—for if it happens, it happens in nature, and is thus natural. What then is left to mean by calling something "unnatural"?

Well perhaps we mean that it isn't the norm, or that it happens infrequently. But surely we don't want to say that just because something is rare or uncommon that it is somehow wrong or problematic. Diamonds are rare. So is true love. So is snow in southern Texas. So, again it seems it is not clear what we even mean when we say that suicide is wrong because it is unnatural, for we've not gained any clear sense of what that word means, other than perhaps that we don't like it. But that, so far, seems to be just prejudice on our part. (Notice that the same points apply when people try to argue that homosexuality is wrong because it is unnatural: what do we even mean when we talk about things being natural or unnatural?)

Finally, on (2), we might try to argue that suicide is unnatural because it goes against the order that God has set up or established. That, however, is our (3), and so we should examine it as well.

Regarding (3): Remember, (3) says that suicide is wrong because it is offensive to God, and it is offensive in being disruptive of God's plan. As with (3) we will have to understand what it means to speak of God's plan in the first place. Note, first, though, how odd it would be to say that we humans actually were capable of disrupting God's plan. For surely, on traditional western understandings of God, God is an all-powerful being. As such we would expect that God could certainly intervene and prevent anything from happening that s/he didn't want to. So how is it even possible to disrupt God's plan?

Now you might think that the issue isn't so much whether we could truly disrupt God's plan, but that suicide seeks or attempts to. But now we arrive at one of Hume's most important points. Someone who is arguing that suicide is wrong because it is disruptive (or attempts to be) of God's plan and is thus disrespectful of God, perhaps thinks that the problem is that we're trying to make a decision about life and death that is not ours to make. We are, on this view, thought to be trying to interfere with the course of nature that God has devised—the way that God wants the world to be, from one event to the next, and that suicide is trying to violate that series of events or the grand plan for us that God has established.

Now step back from this debate for a moment and consider the following example. You are walking down the street, and you see a bus coming straight at you. If you don't move you will be likely killed by that bus. Would you move out of the way if you could? Of course. But aren't you, in this scenario, trying to avoid what the world seems to have in store for you? There was the bus, coming right at you. So it seems like what was planned was that you get hit by the bus. But you moved. Of course you did. But in doing so, weren't you trying to avoid what the world seemed to have in store for you? That is, acting in a way to save our lives very often seems to be going against what nature looks to have in store for us. In fact, we do that all the time, whenever we take an aspirin for a headache, or have surgery to fix an ailment, or build a dam to change the flow of a river. Those are all cases where we seem to be interfering with God's plans (or the plans of nature). But we don't think we are doing something wrong when we jump out of the way of the bus, or take an aspirin, or have surgery to cure an ailment or disease.

In fact, don't we often think that what the right thing to do in many of these cases is to explicitly fight against what nature and the world seems to have in store for us? But, and this is the key point: If it is OK to interfere with nature's apparent plans in order to preserve our life, why would it be wrong to end our lives? We've seen that just interfering with nature's (or God's) plan isn't wrong in general. So why would it be wrong in the case of suicide?

In this chapter we've asked lots of difficult questions. That is not a surprise, given how complicated and controversial the topic of suicide is. The moral of our investigation might best be put as that we've not necessarily answered all of the important questions. But we have figured out what some of the important questions are to be asking. That itself can count as progress, as we at least know how to begin thinking more clearly about such a difficult topic.

CHAPTER 8

Distributive Justice

What Is Government For?

When you think about the concept of justice, you very well may have something like a courtroom in mind, where verdicts are read out that may be just or unjust. Or, relatedly, you might think of whether justice was done (or "served") in a given situation, say by a trial, or whether a person or people suffered injustices through historical wrongdoings, or whether someone convicted of a crime received a just sentence. We also speak of "miscarriages of justice" when we think someone guilty got away with a terrible crime. That is to say, when you think about justice you may have in mind what we would more clearly label as "criminal justice," the kind studied by lawyers, sociologists, or criminologists. But that isn't the only way we speak of justice. In fact, Plato's most famous dialogue, *The Republic*, is devoted to exploring the nature of justice and its various facets, from just societies to just actions to even whether a person's soul is just or not.

Despite the importance of these various meanings and uses of the concept of justice, in this chapter we are going to explore a different sense entirely. This will be justice as it refers in general to how governments are structured or organized, and how they should behave. More specifically, we will explore justice as it relates to the distribution of things like money, power, opportunity, and even freedoms and liberties. Asking about how such things, what we will call "social goods," are distributed, and how they should be distributed in a society, will help us address some of the most fundamental and important questions in political philosophy. We will be asking, that is, about what constitutes a just society, where the focus is on how those social goods are distributed among the citizens of that society. Questions about criminal justice, sentencing, punishment, and the like, will have to wait for another occasion.

As we'll see, to inquire into how things such as money and power should be distributed in a just society will be tied to questions about how societies should be organized, what role governments have, and what (if anything) makes governments legitimate. Such questions are tied to debates that we often find in the news, namely questions about how big government should be, and what its function is. Though we will start with a view about government that dates back to the seventeenth century philosopher, Hobbes, we will find ourselves talking about questions and debates that are still very much alive today.

To start with a very large question, what do you think the purpose or function of government is? Starting with that question will help pave the way for our discussion about what might be called "distributive justice"—how those social goods we listed ought to be distributed in a society that we think is a just society. Hobbes wrestled with the question of the role and importance of government, no doubt partly as a response to the English Civil War of the seventeenth century.

To see what the role of government is, we might begin be imagining how things would be in the absence of a government, either because of war or famine or environmental calamities. In such a world without government it seems there would be no rules for people to follow, and certainly no governing body around to enforce any rules that had previously existed. It seems that every person would be left to fend for themselves. Of course most of us are not capable of surviving truly by ourselves, without help from others. But if there were no government and no institutions such as courts, or police, or banks, each of us would be in an extremely vulnerable position, where perhaps only the strongest would survive, but even the strongest might not be able to do everything needed to really survive. If you found yourself in such a situation, what would you do?

Well, given that none of us is truly, entirely self-sufficient, you might expect that people would form pacts or agreements with others, where people would for starters promise to not steal from and kill one another. It would be in our self-interest, it seems, to promise to not harm another in return for a promise from another that they wouldn't harm us. This is perhaps the meager starting point for all societies and governments—a mutual agreement among people to refrain from harming each other. Each of us, perhaps, thinking about what is best for ourselves, would want the maximum amount of freedom to do what we want, where the limit of our freedom would be to not act in ways that harm others, or more generally, to not interfere with other people's pursuits, so long as they don't interfere with ours.

We can think of this as a kind of agreement we might make among ourselves were we in a situation with no government. In fact, Hobbes thought this kind of agreement so important he gave it a name, "the social contract." Now this "contract" raises lots of important questions, say about how it works, about whether people need to explicitly agree to it in order to be bound by it, etc. For our purposes we can immediately turn to asking about what the point of government is at all, having started with this idea that people without a government, left to fend for themselves, would agree to the terms of such a contract (e.g., I won't kill you so long as you don't kill me).

The answer is not hard to find, for surely we want to make sure that this agreement among our government-less individuals is kept. We need something powerful enough to make sure everyone is keeping the promises or contracts we've formed with others, and powerful enough to punish those who break the promises or contracts. And that, it seems, is the first legitimate role for government we've found: to be the overseer and enforcer of contracts, otherwise staying out of the way of people's freely chosen pursuits, where, again, such pursuits are OK so long as they don't interfere with another's desired pursuit.

A View from the Right: Minimalist Views of Government

Let us, following a famous American philosopher of the twentieth century, Robert Nozick, give a name to a view which holds that government's job is solely to play this role of enforcer of promises and contracts. We'll call it the "night watchman" view of government. By that we mean that government's job is to simply enforce the contracts and agreements we've made, and to protect us from those who would seek to break such contracts by stealing our property, causing bodily harm to any of us, etc. Nozick is said to fall on the "right" of the political spectrum within American politics, where by that we'll mean simply that he advocates for a minimal role for government—the role of night watchman. That is, Nozick, as we'll see later in more detail, is not concerned with ensuring that people have the same amount of those social goods we mentioned, but merely with keeping us safe and enforcing contracts. Within the economic realm, Nozick is advocating the famous policy of laissez-faire (which literal means "hands off") where the point is that government's job is to simply ensure that people don't rip each other off, commit fraud, or in other ways engage in problematic deceptions of others. That market, it is said, is left to its own devices, producing winners and losers, but not, importantly, weighing in on how economic or social goods should actually be distributed.

We will return to this view of Nozick's but for now it might help to explain it a bit more by contrasting it with the other view we'll examine, one by the famous philosopher John Rawls. Rawls can be thought of as endorsing a more "leftish" political philosophy, the kind most usually associated with the Democratic Party in the United States. On Rawls' view, the government has a much greater role to play than just Nozick's night watchman view, as it is also supposed to play a role in how social goods such as opportunity, wealth, power, etc., are in fact distributed within a given society. So far then we have the outlines of two very different visions for the role of government, with Nozick advocating a small, limited role, while Rawls advocates a much more involved and robust role for government. Exploring each view in more detail, with an eye to deciding which is better will be the goal for the remainder of this chapter.

We'll begin with Nozick's advocacy for small government. How, in particular, does Nozick think social goods should be distributed? What does Nozick value when it comes to the distribution of these goods, and what role should the government have in that distribution? Well, according to Nozick, if we are trying to determine whether a distribution of social goods is a just distribution we need to examine how the distribution came to be. We can think of this as a historical-based emphasis, for it says that a distribution is *unjust* only when the process of distributing goods has gone wrong in either of two ways. The point of focusing on the process or the history will be in stark contrast to Rawls' approach. Rawls, as we'll see, thinks the key question is how the goods are in fact distributed, where he doesn't mean the process of distributing them, but the result. Nozick focuses only on the process.

What processes of distributing social goods matter for Nozick? He thinks we need to look at what he calls (a) transfer in holdings—namely how one person came to trade their social goods for others, or more generally, what are the mechanisms for getting social goods from one person or institution to another. Typically, in the kind of society Nozick is thinking of, namely one that is market driven—that is, capitalism—it is by free economic activity that we transfer our holdings among ourselves. For instance, you own two cows. I have a bundle of money but no cows, though I'd like to start raising cattle. So, you and I agree to trade—I give you a portion of my money and in exchange you give me the cows. So long as I didn't give you counterfeit money, and you didn't mislead me about the age or breed or health of the cows, we'll make our trade and go our separate ways. Government has no role to play here, other than ensuring there are open markets that allow for such trade, and that no one is prevented from engaging in such economic activity. You get your money, in this case, from the portion I had. I, in turn, got that portion of money by trading or by selling something, or being paid for my labor by somebody else. And that person got the money to pay me by, for instance, building a factory that I work at, where I exchange my labor for money (say, an hourly wage). So far, so good.

Now if we think about this ongoing series of economic transfers we notice, to simplify, that one person gets their holdings (their portion of those social goods we've been referring to) from another, and that person gets there's from a different person, who in turn got them from someone else, etc. Eventually, it seems, there has to be someone or some group of people who got the whole chain started by *originally* acquiring those valuables. This, historically, has usually been the acquiring of land, which people used to grow things that they sold, and the whole process gets started. So, in other words, another place we'd want to keep an eye out for an *injustice* would be in the *acquiring* of social goods.

Any injustice, according to Nozick, in the distribution of social goods would have had to occur in either:

a)   The transfer of holdings (i.e., social goods) or
b)   The acquisition of these social goods.

Now so long as there is no injustice in either of these two parts of the history of holdings (acquiring and transferring) there is no injustice to be found. And here's the key part: So long as there's not injustice in either (a) or (b), the end result doesn't matter. That is, so long as there was no injustice (by theft, or deceit, or fraud, etc.) in the process, it does not matter how social goods end up distributed. It doesn't matter if the top .001% of a wealthy nation own 40, 50, 60, or 99% of all the social goods. The resultant distribution doesn't count as unjust so long as the process was just. As such, there is no room for government to get involved.

How does government get involved, in most countries, in keeping the amount of social goods from being too unevenly distributed? By taxation. Taxation, that is, is the mechanism governments use to re-distribute social goods, to ensure that that there isn't too much disparity or difference among people. But for someone like Nozick, taxation isn't legitimate, as it involves a redistribution of social goods even when the process hasn't involved a violation of (a) or (b).

Nozick, in fact, goes so far as to say that taxes, taking a portion of your paycheck, say, amounts to forcing you to work for free—namely, the hours you worked but didn't get paid because some of your pay was withheld from you.

Now there is one important exception to all of this. As you might expect, if we were to discover that there has been an injustice in either the *acquisition* or the *transfer* of social goods, then taxation would be appropriate, to return things to the state they would be in were it not for that violation. But, according to Nozick, that is the only time taxation is legitimate. Before we continue, you should pause to consider how radical a view that really is. Nobody likes to pay taxes, but Nozick thinks they are worse than just undesired—he thinks it involves something immoral (again, unless they are being used to correct an injustice in acquisition or transfer of those social goods).

A View from the Left: Substantial Views of Government

We now turn to Rawls' position, which I said above envisions a greater role for government, including the use of taxes to redistribute social goods. And for Rawls, such redistribution is needed not only when there has been something illegal or unjust in the acquiring or transferring of social goods, but in many more situations. What Rawls uses to help make this point is one of the most famous examples in contemporary philosophy.

As we saw, Rawls thinks the place to look for injustice isn't only in the places that Nozick says, but also in the resulting distribution of those social goods—who has what and what level of inequality there is. Now, contrary to what you might expect, Rawls does not think that justice requires that everyone have exactly the same amount of social goods. He does think that some inequality in the distribution of social goods is acceptable but only if it meets a certain condition, one he calls "the difference principle." We'll work our way up to explaining what Rawls means by this "difference principle," by starting with some important points Rawls makes to help guide us as we think about what justice involves.

First, when we try to think about what policies should govern taxes, say, or how social goods should be distributed, we need to be as impartial as we can, not letting our own social position or wealth influence our views about what is just. After all, it is only natural that we would be biased toward policies that would benefit us. So, for instance, if you were incredibly wealthy it would be easy to imagine you more sympathetic toward policies that would perhaps have lower tax rates on the rich. If we were trying to come up with an account of justice that was truly fair to everyone, then we'd need to find a way to eliminate such biases, including ones we might not even be aware of in ourselves.

Second, continuing in the tradition from Hobbes, Rawls is going to have us approach issues of justice by imagining that people are motivated solely by self-interest. This is an important point that is easily forgotten, especially if you watch political debates on TV or read about them in the news. People on the left side of the political spectrum (in the United States, typically, the Democratic Party) are often said to be guided or motivated by a concern for others (hence the pejorative term, "bleeding heart liberal"), as if that is the only way to justify or motivate policies that have a greater role for government than those on the right would advocate. But that is not Rawls' approach, and he will begin with the same starting point as many in what's come to be known as "classic liberalism"—a tradition of thinking about the nature of government and the role it should play in people's lives—where the key, again, is that we imagine people to be motivated solely by a concern by what is best for themselves.

Rawls takes these two points and puts them together in a famous kind of thought experiment. Let us imagine that you and a group of people are trying to decide which principles should govern the distribution of social goods in your society. Should there be taxes? Should there be a government? What powers should it have? In order to ensure that our own biases don't creep into our deliberations, Rawls has us imagine that we are, in his words, "behind the veil of ignorance." By that he means that we are to imagine ourselves, in this process of deliberating about which principles would be just ones, to lack any knowledge about our own particular wealth, social status, family history, and even any information about our own potential to acquire social goods. We need to deliberate without any of the information that might bias ourselves, and that state of lack of knowledge is what he's getting at in this image of the "veil of ignorance."

Suppose then that you know nothing about your own prospects or how much wealth you have or stand to inherit or any of those kinds of details. Imagine you have some knowledge about how capitalism in general works, and about markets and the like, but not about where you stand in a given society. And imagine you are trying to think of policies that will best suit you, even though you don't know any details about your own situation. Which policies would you choose?

Rawls thinks the first set of policies or principles we'd select, as rational, self-interested individuals, would be similar to what Nozick favors—namely that we be as free from outside interference as possible, and that we thus have as much freedom as we can, compatible with others' freedom, to pursue the things we value and want. But that's not all, says Rawls.

He thinks that we'd also want to ensure that our society was set up in a way that would guarantee that those worst off would be in the best position that would be possible for them. Why? Because not knowing where we actually are in the hierarchy of who has what and how much, we would recognize that we ourselves could very well be among those who are worst off when it comes to those social goods. Most people aren't rich, after all, and so it is more likely than not that we wouldn't be among those who have lots. Since we are acting out of self-interest, we'd want to make sure that even those at the bottom don't completely sink, for that might be where we find ourselves. Rawls thinks we'd play it safe, in other words, and not gamble on our being among the lucky few, instead choosing policies that would protect us if we found ourselves at the bottom, not at the top.

This idea, to protect those at the bottom, is what the "difference principle" is driving at. It holds that inequalities among social goods can be acceptable, so long as the inequality makes those at the bottom better off than they would be if everything were equally divided. How could that be? Well, imagine we let people who study and work hard make more than others. That could provide incentive for people to become doctors, for instance. And if there are doctors, they could help those not just at the top but also at the bottom. And if there are doctors and others making more money than some, that extra economic activity they are responsible for could actually help drive an economy as a whole to do better, which in turn could make those at the bottom better off than they would be otherwise, say where no one had incentives to work hard.

Now, importantly, Rawls isn't demanding that everyone have the same amount of social goods. There can be unequal distributions. But there is a limit. For such inequalities have to actually benefit those at the bottom. And if economic activity creates a situation where people at the bottom are not being made better, then a redistribution of those economic goods will be required. Taxes, that is to say, are likely to be needed, to both help those at the bottom, and to be used when levels of inequality become too great. But remember, this idea about helping those at the bottom be better off than they would be otherwise is not being driven by our hoping people will care about those at the bottom. Instead, Rawls thinks we'd agree that this is how things should be set up because we ourselves might very well find ourselves at the bottom. Thus the true principles of justice, are the ones that we would agree to when we are behind that veil of ignorance. The difference principle, in particular, would be one we'd chose because it is in own self-interest to do so.

If we step back and compare Rawls' and Nozick's views, we can see how much they disagree on. For where Nozick will think of taxation as an unacceptable violation of people's freedom, Rawls will view it as necessary to ensure a society that is fair and just.

Justice and Fairness

Rawls describes his view about distributive justice as "justice as fairness," and so it is worth enquiring into what he means by "fairness." One thing we can note is that when we treat people fairly we treat them equally. We might put that into practice by making sure that our society, the one drawn up or imagined by those behind the veil of ignorance, is one that does not discriminate against others, one where everyone has equal opportunity for success. We might think of this as what some philosophers call "negative liberty," which is to say we value freedom or liberty, and we strive to make sure there is not interference from others as a person seeks out a job or an education. We call this "negative" not because it is bad, but simply to indicate that we mean by it that people are to be left alone, and not interfered with. This would be in contrast to a society that takes positive means to help people achieve their goals.

Consider this example. Imagine two people, one quite wealthy and one quite poor. The first comes from a family where everyone has gone to college, and the family has the financial mean to finance their child's education, so that that child doesn't end up with any college loans or debts. The second person's family is poor, with no one in the family ever having attended college. The family also doesn't have the resources to pay or assist for their child to go to college.

Now step back and think about these two people. Are they both free to go to college? Well, in one sense, yes. There is no law that would prevent either from attending college, and they are free to submit applications and to go if they are accepted. That is, there is no interference from without, and so we might say they both have the "negative freedom" to go to college. But you also might think that there's an important sense in which they are not on equal footing. After all, if someone lacks the resources for paying for college, has no role models to follow, and has been raised in an environment where going to college isn't valued, that person's genuine opportunity to go to college is very different from the first wealthy person.

How might Rawls think about this situation, so as to guarantee genuine equal opportunity? Well one important part of his view is that it is wrong to penalize people for things that are not their fault. Just as we shouldn't reward people's successes if they didn't earn them, we shouldn't make people suffer for factors beyond their control. If we are truly going to treat people fairly, we have to make sure that people aren't being penalized for things that aren't their fault.

In the college example, one might argue that the wealthy child is benefiting from advantages that he had no role in creating—he just happened to be born into wealth; just as the poor child just happened to be born into poverty. In neither case did the individual bring about the circumstances that will shape how their lives unfold. And arguably the poor person we're speaking of has a much harder road to climb, even though they've done nothing to deserve that.

Now you might say, "Well, life isn't fair, and that's just the way things are." And while it may be true that life isn't fair in the sense that people are often dealt difficult hands, while others are born lucky, we might think that the whole point of a society—one that values justice and fairness—is to minimize where possible the unfairness life delivers. Perhaps, then, it is actually the job of society to create genuine opportunities for people to succeed. That it isn't enough to simply stand back and watch things play out, with some benefiting from things they didn't earn while others suffer for factors beyond their control. If you think it is wrong to simply do nothing, you might have to reimagine the role of government as one that also has the duty to level the playing field where it can. And unlike Nozick's view, as we've seen, this will no doubt require a greater role for government in people's lives.

As a final point, when thinking about this college example, imagine yourself back behind the veil of ignorance, not knowing whether your family has the resources to send you to college. What policy would you adopt? Would you want to make sure there is more than just "negative liberty"? More than just the absence of discrimination? Would you want your society to be one that gives people genuine opportunities to succeed, and in that way operates to ensure true fairness? That, at least, becomes a pressing question as we try to determine exactly what is fair and what role government should have in ensuring a just society.

CHAPTER 9

Personal Identity

Identity and Time

What makes you the particular person you are? What, that is, makes you *you*? We tend to think that each of us is a unique individual, and even if we had an identical twin, we'd still be the particular person we are, unique, and one of a kind. So what is it that makes you the unique individual you are? In this chapter we'll look at several different answers that have been proposed. We'll need a bit of terminology to help, so we'll start there.

The question we started with was about what makes you the person you are. That can be understood as a question about what makes you the individual you are at a specific time. We'll call that "synchronic identity"—which just means we are talking about your identity—who you are as a unique individual at a given time. But we'll also want to know what makes you the particular person you are over a period of time or at different times. For even though you may go through changes, such as cutting your hair, or losing weight, you very well are the same person after the changes as you were before. That will be what we call "diachronic identity"—your identity as the same person at different times.

Next, we have to be careful when we use the word "same." I've spoken so far about your being the same person at one time as you are at another. But the word "same" can have different meanings, and it is crucial to this discussion that we keep them straight. Think of identical twins. They can be said to be the same. But the way they are the same is different from what we mean when we say you are the same person at different times. What's going on here is that when we are talking about identical twins, we mean that they are "qualitatively identical"—the same in having all of their qualities in common. At a given time, we can imagine numerous things having the same qualities, and we would therefore say of them that they are qualitatively identical (the same).

Contrast that with another way in which we speak of something being the same or identical. You, at age nineteen, are the same person you were when you were ten. In this case we know that you are not qualitatively identical at those different times, as you are taller now, or have a different haircut, different clothes, etc. But you are still the same person. And by that we mean you are one and the same individual at those different times. There's only one of you, and the person that existed at age ten is one and the same person who is now nineteen. We'll use the term "numerically identical" when speaking of this kind of identity.

To put those pieces of terminology to work, we can say things like: You are numerically identical at different times (diachronic identity) even though you are not qualitatively identical at those different times. Likewise, even though two twins may be qualitatively identical, they are still two different beings, and thus are not numerically identical. There are two of them, after all, not one. Qualitative identity, we might say, is not enough to guarantee numerical identity. And when talking about identity over time, numerical identity doesn't require qualitative identity.

We can now use those terms and distinctions to make clearer what we are asking about in this chapter. First, we can ask what makes you the particular person you are at a given time. Second, we can ask what makes you the same person (numerically identical) at different times. It is this second question we will spend more time on. What, then, explains your identity over time?

The Soul Criterion

Many people think of themselves as a kind of combination of different fundamental elements: a physical body on the one hand, and something non-physical or immaterial on the other. Different words have been used to name that non-physical part of you. Let's just call it your "soul," as that is a fairly common expression. If asked what makes you the particular person you are at a given time (synchronic identity), you might want to answer that it is the presence of a unique soul that makes you the person you are. Perhaps your soul is the ground of all of your personality traits and character, your values and nature. Likewise, you might want to argue that it is the presence of the same (numerically speaking) soul at different times that makes you identical over time.

That is, you have the same particular soul at one time, and that very same particular soul is present at a later time. It is thus the identity of your soul (one soul at different times) that explains how you are the same person from one time to the next.

Many famous philosophers have argued that this is a way to think about your identity— both at a single time and over time. But this view also has a number of serious objections to deal with. I'll list a few, and leave it to you to see if you can come up with a response on behalf of the "soul criterion of identity."

First, by the very definition of souls, they are immaterial and thus not perceivable by the senses. That makes it perhaps impossible for anyone to identity a soul. And while we could take this point and begin to ask whether we have reasons to think that souls even exist, we will instead pursue a different line of questioning. For notice, second, that if souls are not perceivable, it seems that we have no way of verifying that the soul present in you at one time is one and the same soul (numerically identical) at a different time. If a soul makes you who you are, and if there are different souls present in you at different times, that would mean you are a different person at different times. Thus the only way to ensure that you are same person from one time to another would be to somehow verify that you have the same particular soul at those different times. But that seems impossible to do, given that souls can't be observed, measured, or kept track of. We don't, in other words, have a way of ruling out the possibility that different souls are trading places in you at different times. But that would be needed if we wanted to be sure you were the same person from one time to another.

We can actually use that same point about souls being unobservable to make a more sophisticated argument against using souls as the source of your identity over time. The argument goes like this:

1) We make reliable, accurate judgments all the time about whether a person is the same person from one time to the next.
2) If what made a person the same over time was the presence of an identical soul, then our judgments about someone's identity over time would require verifying that the same soul was present at different times.

3) Souls, however, are unobservable, and thus no one is able to verify that the same soul exists at different times.

4) If we were indeed relying on accurate judgments about identical souls over time, then we would not truly know if a person was the same person over time.

5) But we do know whether someone is the same person over time.

6) Therefore it must not be souls that we are relying on to judge the identity of a person over time.

The point of this argument isn't to show that souls don't exist. Rather, it designed to show that even if they did exist, we don't (and can't) rely on them to help us make judgments about a person's identity over time. They are doing no work in helping us make what we take to be accurate judgments about a person's diachronic identity. We don't rely on them, in other words, and so they don't seem to be doing much philosophical work when it comes to explaining identity over time. And if they are doing no work, we don't stand to lose anything by ceasing to speak of or theorize about them.

The Body Criterion

Now you might think that the way to reply to the above is to say that while we don't judge directly that the same soul is present from one time to another, we do so indirectly, by looking to see if the same physical body is present at one time and then at another. This can help the soul criterion only if we know, however, that there is a correlation—that the same soul always sticks with the same body, and so if we see the same body at different times we know that the same soul must be present.

That sounds pretty good, until we ask how we know that there is that correlation of same body with same soul. If we can't inspect or observe a soul, what gives us any reason to think that the same physical body retains the same soul over time? Couldn't different, but qualitatively similar souls occupy a body at different times? If that happens we again would find ourselves forced to say that it is not the same person from one time to another. The unobservable nature of souls has created problems again.

Perhaps then we should try something different, and opt for a view that takes seriously the observation we just made: we seem to judge the same person exists at different times by looking to see if the same physical body is present. True, that physical body can change over time, but we've already discussed how numerical identity is consistent with changes in a thing's qualitative nature. Different qualities at different times doesn't mean we have two different things, as one thing can simply change (some) of its qualities over time and still be the same thing.

Maybe that is the answer then: what makes you the same person from one time to another is that you have the same physical body (even though that body will undergo changes from one time to another.) So here, again, the idea is: same body = same person. This would be the "body criterion of a person's identity." Can it, though, stand up to scrutiny?

Here's a thought experiment intended to show that the body criterion is not a suitable answer—you are not your body, and the presence of the same body over time does not ensure that you have survived as the same particular person over time.

Imagine two people, person A and person B, sitting in a laboratory. Now imagine that person A has their brain removed and put into the person B's head, while person B has their brain put into person A's body. Now ask yourself: If you were person A, when you opened your eyes after the brain switching, where would you expect to find yourself? If the body criterion were correct, then you, person A, would expect to open your eyes and find your familiar body, that of person A. But I don't think that is what you'd expect to experience. Instead, it is likely that you would imagine yourself waking up in a strange new body, namely that of person B. You would still be around but you would have a different body now. In other words, it seems as if you go where your brain goes, not where your body does. And that seems enough to help us conclude that the body criterion of identity is not adequate.

But let us think through this idea that you go where you brain goes a bit more carefully. While your intuitions likely make you think that it is your brain that is essential to making you who you are, and that it is the same brain over time that would make for you being the same person over time. But this brain of yours is something you've never seen. More importantly, though, is the question about what about the brain is so special, that lets us say same brain = same person. Is what matters about your brain the particular lump of squishy grey matter, matter that you have never seen or experienced? Or, instead, is it not just the stuff, the matter of your brain which is crucial, but rather, all the information that is contained in that brain—your memories, your thoughts, your personality traits? In short, it seems what matters when it comes to the brain is all of the information that is stored there—just like what matters in your computer isn't the particular pile of metal and plastic, but rather all the information stored. That's why we make back-ups of our computer, isn't it? Because what matters is the information stored, not the particular physical laptop or desktop.

And so it seems with our brains as well—it is the information contained within that we want to be maintained. And that leads us away from the body criterion of identity and moves us to yet another possible account of what makes you the person you are, at a single time and over a period of time.

The Psychological Criterion of Identity

As we've seen, what seems to matter most when it comes to our identity is all of the information contained in our brains, not the particular lump of grey matter that sits between our ears. What kind of information do we care about, that would help ensure that we are the same person from one time to another? Here we might talk about "psychological continuity." By that we mean that there are connections between the various stages of your life: that you remember events from an earlier time, that you are now carrying out projects that an earlier stage had intended to do, that your personality stays constant over time. Those are the psychological traits that both make you who you are, and the important kinds of information that you would want to survive.

Think about someone who has undergone a terrible brain injury such that they can no longer remember anything from their past, whose personality has undergone a radical change, and who values completely different things. There is an important sense in which that person is no longer the same person they were before. Sure, their body might still be present, but if their psychological traits were sufficiently different, we would find ourselves saying, in more than a mere metaphorical sense, that this is not the same person we knew before. A different person is now present.

Another way to think about it is from the first-person. If you awoke one day, with no memories of the past, unable to even recognize familiar people from your life, you very well might conclude that though you may still share the same body as a person that existed before this global amnesia, that you just are not identical to that person. What seems to be needed to retain your identity over time is bundles of memories that help sustain a rich psychological continuity with a person that existed previously. And so on this view, it is the bundle of memories, hopes, goals, values, character, etc., which when preserved over time allows us to say you are numerically identical with the person who also shares those psychological features, that is, previous stages of your life. Those two stages are part of the same person because of the psychological continuity between those stages.

Duplication (Fission) Cases

So far it seems that what we called the "psychological criterion" of personal identity has the best claim on making you the person you are at a given time, and the same person over time. We now look at a famous science-fiction example that creates a puzzle for that psychological criterion.

Remember that we said that what seems to matter was not your body, but your brain. But when we looked more closely, it was the information in your brain that matters, not the physical stuff. And we drew a parallel with computers. So long as your data is present and retained over time, your computer has survived over time. But when we start thinking about the data or information that is stored in your brain a funny puzzle arises.

Imagine that scientists have found a way to capture and store all the information contained in your brain—your memories, personality, etc. And let us imagine they have figured out a way to let you travel to Mars, though not in the traditional sense of transporting your body. Instead, you step into a tele-transporter, which scans all the information in your brain, and sends that information to another tele-transporter on Mars. The person on Earth is physically destroyed after the data has been gathered and sent to Mars. On Mars, that data is "uploaded" into a physical body. If you walked into the tele-transporter on Earth, your experience might be something like: You walk into the transporter, and are given a drug to make you fall asleep. The information from your brain is sent to Mars, and the body on Mars, with all of that information now placed into the brain on Mars is awoken from its own sleep. For you, you start on Earth, fall asleep, and then wake up on Mars, as all the information that is you is in that brain on Mars. The body and brain on Earth is destroyed, but you survive as the same particular person, now on Mars. So far so good it seems.

But imagine that there is a glitch. You step into the transporter, the information is sent to Mars where it is placed in a body that is there. But something goes wrong and the body and brain on Earth is not destroyed. Instead the person on Earth has all that information that makes you who you are. And so does the person on Mars. After the scientists scramble to figure out what has happened, they decide to let the person on Earth and the person on Mars speak to each other by phone. The key question now, though, is: Which person are you? When the machine was working, you assumed that you simply were sent to Mars, and survived as the identical person you were on Earth. So in this glitch-scenario, you are now on Mars, just as before. But because of the glitch you are now on Earth as well. It seems that now you could talk to yourself. But if you try to imagine where you are, where would you expect to wake up? On Earth? On Mars? On both places? But imagining you are in two places at once seems impossible.

Put a bit more precisely, the person on Earth before the transport, A, is identical to the person who awakens on Mars, who we will call B. And so A = B. But when the glitch happens, the person on Earth who enters the transporter is also the same person who exits it—call that person C. So, A = C. And if A and B are the same, and A and C are the same, then it seems to follow that B and C are the same. But B and C are not one person, they are two—one on Mars and one on Earth. That is, there are two of you. But identity is something that only one thing can have with one thing—two different things can't be the same particular thing. Yet that is exactly what has happened. So not only do we have the puzzle of where you'd expect to find yourself, we also have this logical puzzle, of two distinct beings allegedly being a single being. That's a problem. And so as promising as the psychological criterion of identity seemed to be, it looks to allow for this unsolvable puzzle. And because it leads to such an intractable puzzle, it seems right to conclude that something in the psychological criterion is problematic. But what? And how do we fix the problem?

CHAPTER 10

Language and Experience

Linguistic Determinism

Philosophers have long been interested in the nature of perception. For perception is where our minds make contact with the world. And many have thought that the knowledge we have of the world is somehow based or grounded in our perceptions of the world—what we see, hear, touch, taste, etc. For a long time philosophers assumed that the world just impinged upon our senses, leaving its stamp on our minds, in the way a stamp leaves its mark on soft wax. If that picture is right, we simply have to examine what those impressions or stamps on our minds are like and we can have knowledge of the world which caused them.

This nice, tidy picture of the relationship between the world and our minds began to be questioned by eighteenth-century philosophers such as Kant. On Kant's view, we are not merely passive recipients of information from the world. Instead, our experience of the world is partly a matter of what information the world gives us, but it is also partly a function of how our minds construct or organize the data that is given to us. Think for a moment about all that you are experiencing at a given moment: there is what you see, what you hear, what you feel, what you smell, etc. That is, there is a huge amount of information that bombards our senses. Perhaps we are able to comprehend and experience the world only because we are taking that raw data that is given to us and organizing it, carving it up into meaningful units that we can then make sense of.

Now Kant's philosophy of experience is incredibly rich, but also complicated. But let's take seriously for the moment the idea that what we experience is partly a result of how we organize the data given to us in experience. Kant thought this was a basic function of how the mind works—imposing structure and order onto our experiences. Later philosophers, inspired by Kant, thought the source of this organization of the raw data of experience wasn't merely a function of our minds, but instead it was a result of language. The language we speak and understand plays a role in organizing the data of experience, and the concepts we have when we can speak a language shape and influence what we experience.

A famous example, one that comes from a twentieth-century philosopher, Wittgenstein, can help make the point more vividly. Consider the following picture:

Courtesy Eric Rubenstein.

Now, if you are a speaker of English, you will most certainly have the concept of "rabbit" and also the concept of "duck." Go back and look at that figure and see it as a rabbit. That is, you can use "rabbit" to influence what you see, and then by switching and thinking about ducks, what you see suddenly changes. The picture of course has stayed the same, but what you experience seems to have changed, depending on how you've organized the lines of the drawing. And what led you to organize them in different ways was simply your using different words from a language you know.

Let us take this rather simple example and turn it into a much more radical and interesting hypothesis. Namely, everything you experience is determined or shaped or structured by the language you speak. What makes that such an interesting and radical hypothesis is not just that it says that your experience is mediated by language, as opposed to the simplistic model of perception we started with. What is really interesting (and controversial) is that if what you experience is the result of the language you speak, then two people who speak completely different languages should experience the world in radically different ways.

Now this is a rather speculative hypothesis about experience and the role of language.

But in the 1950s and 1960s, anthropologists began making some very interesting discoveries as they studied the languages of different cultures. In particular, researchers discovered that some cultures had a much more limited vocabulary of color words than we do. In fact, there are some cultures where there are only three basic color words—white, black, and red. If we take this fact and combine it with the philosophical idea that our experience is shaped by the language we speak we arrive at a fascinating possibility: perhaps speakers of that language of only three basic color words actually see the world radically differently than speakers of English do. Perhaps, that is, everything they see is either white, black, red, or a combination of those. Since they don't have a particular word for blue, for instance, when they look at the sky they wouldn't see what we do. Nor when they look out on a forest or field.

This idea that language shapes or determines our experience such that different languages result in people experiencing radically different worlds is sometimes known as the "Whorf-Sapir Hypothesis," named after two highly influential linguistic sociologists. And the idea that language does play this role of shaping what we experience is what we can call "linguistic determinism."

Time, Language, and Experience

We've touched upon the fascinating idea that people with different color vocabularies may have different visual experiences of the world, literally experiencing different worlds, depending on the resources of their language. Yet it is not only color where we find the possibility of such divergent experiences. For Whorf and Sapir both studied different cultures' understanding of time. What they found is that there are some languages which lack words or concepts for the future, as well as languages which do not have the same level of complexity in the verb-tenses, which again limits their ability to speak of different times, compared with languages such as English. Following again the idea of linguistic determinism, this suggests an even more radical thought: that different cultures might even experience time differently, depending on the language they speak.

For instance, Whorf famously argued that the Hopi culture of northeastern Arizona, seemed to have no words for time as a dimension that exists separate and independent from space. Accordingly, he hypothesized, people speaking Hopi had no experiences of what we might describe as the flow of time—the ongoing, dynamic changes and passage of time that seem such a fundamental part of our experience.

What is so significant about this hypothesis is that it suggests not only that people speaking different languages experience genuinely different worlds, but something even more radical. For if all of our experience of the world is mediated by the language we speak, and language is the only way we have of organizing and structuring the raw data that the world gives to our senses, then it may not be possible to ever know how the world truly is in itself. All anyone ever knows and experiences is colored by the language they speak, with each different language providing a different world of experience. Since it is not possible to step outside our language if we want to experience, understand, and communicate our experiences, we are left with the possibility that we can never know how things truly are in themselves, but only as they appear to us via the language we speak. Nor does it seem possible to determine which, if any, of the various languages used to describe the world is more accurate than another in depicting the way the world is. That's a truly radical, skeptical conclusion about our ability to know our world.

Language, Translation, and Experience

Now if this all sounds too wild and unbelievable to you—that merely speaking different languages can cause people to experience and live in radically different worlds—you might try to show there is something wrong with this line of thought. One way to do that would be to argue that despite the apparent differences among the various languages we've discussed, they still can be translated into each other. After all, Whorf and others are able to report what the speakers of these other languages are saying because they are able to provide accurate translations. And if these languages can be translated into each other, perhaps they are not so different after all. And if they are not so different, we perhaps can avoid the conclusion that speakers of these languages are experiencing different worlds because their languages just *aren't* that different at root.

Now if you really were convinced that different languages lead speakers to experience genuinely different worlds, you will have to deal with this question of translation. Perhaps the best way to do so, if again you are still convinced that different languages can lead to radically different worlds of experience, you'd have to show or make it reasonable to believe that we can find cases of two languages that really cannot be translated into each other. If they can't be translated into each other, then there's not something in common between them, and so speakers of those radically different languages very well might be experiencing different worlds.

Notice how the emphasis has shifted here: we've gone from talking about experience and language to now taking about the possibility (or not) of translating one language from the other. The point at the moment seems to be that to defend the idea that speakers of different languages will experience different worlds we need to find reasons to believe that some languages can't be translated into one another. And while it is a familiar phenomenon that some expressions in one language can't be fully and accurately translated into another language, we're trying to imagine something much more radical—that an entire language can't be translated.

So as our last point in this chapter, let us explore briefly the question of whether it is plausible to imagine one language not being able to be translated into another. Here we face an important problem. And if that problem can't be overcome then the entire captivating idea we started with, namely, that different speakers of different languages could experience different worlds would seem to come crashing down. For if the idea of languages being untranslatable is not tenable, then we've no real reason to think that there really are such radically different languages such that speakers of them wouldn't be able to experience the same world.

What then might make us wary of the idea that there's a language that can't be translated into another? After all, we might imagine societies so far advanced from ours, be they in the future or located somewhere else in the universe, that it is just not possible to translate their language into ours. And perhaps with these different languages they carve the world of experience up in a different way than us.

Imagine you come upon a being who makes noises that you think are a language. But whenever you try to translate their noises, you end up with sentences that seem crazy and false. Your translation manual, as it were, keeps leading you to translate the noises of another as suggesting they experience a radically different view of the world. For example, suppose you build your translation manual, and it leads you to interpret another being as saying "Trees fly and are hatched from blue eggs." Now one way you might go is to decide that you've found a speaker of a language who not only experiences a radically different world than us, and whose words and sentences simply don't make sense. Their sentences don't translate into ours, and when we try we find them saying all kinds of crazy things. So at best they really do experience the world differently, or we are so far from understanding them that we have no idea how they really experience the world. Both of those hypotheses still leave open the possibility of radically different speakers living in very different worlds, ones we may or may not be able to understand.

Now the crucial question is whether you would leave things there—that you've found speakers of a language that doesn't translate into ours in any way which make sense. Perhaps you would conclude that given your best attempts at translation, attempts which show them to have all kinds of crazy beliefs, that you would accept that perhaps they really do experience a radically different world. Perhaps you would. But perhaps you might rethink what has happened. For when we try to translate another person's words and sentences, an overriding rule we follow is that we don't translate people's sentences into sentences that we think are crazy and false. If the translation we come up with make them seem like they have crazy, different beliefs than ours, we would most likely conclude we've not properly translated their words. But what would make us confident that we have translated them correctly? Namely, we would rest assured that we have translated someone's language correctly when we find them to share most of the beliefs we do—and that most of their sentences are true. Some philosophers have called this the "principle of charity," which says that we should always interpret others in a way that gives them the benefit of the doubt.

What's the point of all of this back and forth? Well, if an overriding rule of translating other's sentences is that we find them saying things that we also believe to be true, we will always translate another language in such a way that it carves the world up pretty much like ours. That is, it doesn't seem like we'll ever be able to find evidence of a language that is so radically different from ours that its speakers experience the world differently than we do. And if that is true, the intriguing, even exciting idea we started with—that different languages could result in people experiencing the world radically differently from ours—that idea seems to lose all steam as we'll never find evidence of such a language. For if we do begin to translate another's language in such a way and meet with frustration, what we likely will conclude is simply that we've not yet found the correct way to translate their language. We likely wouldn't conclude they have radically different beliefs, but simply that it is a difficult language to translate. And we would continue to work on it until it finally started to yield sentences that reflected most of our beliefs about how the world is. In the end it seems, we just won't find evidence of others who experience the world radically differently from us, or who speak a language so different from ours that we can't make sense of it, for that will be a sign that our translation job is not finished. It is finished only when their language ends up looking mostly like it is says the same kinds of things about the world as we say.

We seem then to end on a pessimistic note, for when we think about the practical component of translating another's language, it seems we will find everyone pretty much agreeing with the way we experience the world—not necessarily in every detail—but certainly in the major categories and basic structures of the world. The exciting idea that different language speakers could experience radically different worlds seems to just not hold up under scrutiny.

Now, as noted, this seems like a fairly unexciting, even disappointing conclusion to have reached. Maybe there is a mistake contained in the reasoning we have just followed. Maybe that radical thesis still could be defended. The way to do it would be to back up, re-examine the different steps of the arguments deployed. And it would take careful and thorough philosophical examination to achieve that. But, and this is the concluding point of this book: You are now in a position to do just that. For though we began the journey of this book wondering what philosophy is all about, now that we've arrived at the end, you can look back and realize that you actually have been doing philosophy all along. The answers to philosophy's most difficult questions may be hard to resolve. But you now have the start of the tools and training to put you in a position to follow in the footsteps of the great thinkers we've been discussing. And in that way you have become philosophers yourselves, ready to help continue the debates and discussions that have waged for over 2,500 years. And that is a positive note to end on.

CPSIA information can be obtained at www.ICGtesting.com
Printed in the USA
LVOW09s1222020816

498670LV00002B/3/P